EUSTON TO BIRMINGHAM
1837 TO RAIL BLUE

ROBERT HENDRY

AMBERLEY

Front cover, top: The locomotives most associated with the line from Euston in living memory are Stanier 'Duchess' Pacifics in LMS or BR red. Rugby saw them regularly, but they were not Rugby engines, so I was thrilled to film No. 46245 *City of London* in Rugby on a sunny day in 1964; *bottom*: The L&B terminus at Euston featured the Doric arch, which was destroyed to facilitate the new concrete jungle in Euston. Its counterpart in Birmingham had an equally impressive portico but was replaced in the 1850s by New Street as a passenger station. It became a goods and parcels depot, but survived.

Back cover: The London & Birmingham became the London & North Western Railway in 1846. Known as 'the Premier Line', it knew its own importance, timetables reading 'Time Tables of the London & North Western and other railways in connection'. The spine was London to Rugby, where the Birmingham and Trent Valley lines split, the latter for Crewe, Liverpool, Manchester, Carlisle and Glasgow. With artistic licence, the L&B runs like an arrow to Rugby and veers left to Birmingham. Whether trains came from Holyhead, Manchester, Liverpool, Glasgow or Birmingham, they filtered into the L&B, making it the main line to the main lines.

First published 2025

Amberley Publishing
The Hill, Stroud
Gloucestershire, GL5 4EP

www.amberley-books.com

ISBN 978 1 3981 2395 3 (print)
ISBN 978 1 3981 2396 0 (ebook)

British Library Cataloguing in Publication Data.
A catalogue record for this book is available from the British Library.

Typesetting by SJmagic DESIGN SERVICES, India.
Printed in Great Britain.

Appointed GPSR EU Representative:
Easy Access System Europe Oü, 16879218
Address: Mustamäe tee 50, 10621, Tallinn, Estonia
Contact Details: gpsr.requests@easproject.com,
+358 40 500 3575

Contents

Introduction

Some lines gain disproportionate attention such as the Settle–Carlisle line. However, it is easy to see why, with the drama of driving a main line through desolate mountains, fine loco work, superb scenery and sentiment.

The London & Birmingham, often called the first main line railway, was a natural for garnering attention from day one. Commencing from London, unlike the Grand Junction Railway or the Trent Valley, gave it lustre. It was called 'unquestionably the greatest public work ever executed, either in ancient or modern time'. The driving of 112½ miles of railway from Euston to Curzon Street in Birmingham, as New Street station did not exist at that time, was a herculean task.

By the 1830s, the disdain with which parliamentarians had treated the ill-spoken and barely literate George Stephenson had evaporated in face of his early colliery engines, the Stockton & Darlington and Liverpool & Manchester projects. Stephenson's son, Robert, was well educated and, thanks to George's determination, seen as the even more brilliant son of a brilliant father. It was Robert who, with George's approval, became engineer-in-chief of the L&B. The chairman of the L&B from 1837 was George Carr Glyn, the son of a banker and former Lord Mayor of London, and partner in Glyn Mills bank. A popular liberal politician who was returned to Parliament unopposed five times, Glyn knew the top people and was seen as a safe pair of hands, so was a perfect foil for Robert Stephenson.

Together Glyn and Stephenson sought to build an important main line which would impress by its grandeur. This was not showing off, as some thought. Many people were fearful of the new-fangled railways. If they were reassured, it would make the project less threatening. In pre-Victorian Britain, a classical education was the hallmark of respectability. To those who feared railways, the solid magnificence of Hardwick's Doric arch at Euston was a grandiloquent gesture in stone intended to build confidence. Numerous books appeared as the line was being built, one of the best being *Osborne's London & Birmingham Railway Guide*. The preface to one edition of the guide stated:

> Many who, but a few years since, scarcely penetrated beyond the county in which they happened to be born, are now induced to visit places far more remote, from the facility and comfort afforded them by railway transit, which enables them to travel thousands of miles with greater personal ease than they formerly could over fifty. Thus they are brought into contact with numerous individuals in various parts of the kingdom, and become acquainted with customs, manners and habits which previously were wholly unknown to them. The result of this mutual communication of facts and ideas must be an improved state of society. The prejudices and superstitions which have long held sway in the more retired localities, will be swept away before the flood of knowledge which will now pour in upon them.

Most people could not read or write. Travel was too expensive for the 'lower orders', but it was a start on improving society, as Osborne commented. If the more educated and affluent benefitted the most, the benefits would eventually trickle down. The grandeur of the Doric arch was reassuring to those educated in the glories of ancient Rome and Greece. The senators of Rome and the philosophers of Greece invented 'civilisation' and were worthy men, so the new railway age used such familiar props to demonstrate its respectability.

Steam locomotives, by their newness, were strange, but the architectural glories of Rome or Athens were familiar to the educated members of society. Nowadays, we would call them opinion-makers or trendsetters. The seeming extravagance of this voyage into classics, which in reality had nothing to anchor it, as there were no ancient Greek or Roman train stations, was based on association with what was familiar to the educated orders, and so by default reassuring.

Osborne's guide does not mention another factor: prejudice existed around the idea that railways would let the lower orders travel, which would be unsettling for them. If exposure to new habits and manners was good for their betters, similar exposure for the lower orders should elevate them. We like to believe that what is good for us will be good for lesser beings.

The need to reassure was not stressed in the 1830s, let alone today, but was key in what people with a classical education such as Glyn felt was vital. It is hard to project our minds back to such a different world, but they were probably right.

When I was an undergraduate, I had a 'Beermingum gerl friend'. She came from a poor part of Aston with joke schools. She spoke 'Brummmie' rather than English, but it did not make her inferior or bad. She was a delightful girl and meeting her taught me a great deal. If I benefitted from wider horizons in 1970, the visionary ideas of Osborne make sense. This approach is necessary as it allows us to understand what Glyn, Hardwick and Stephenson were doing and makes sense of their actions. The Doric arch at Euston and its counterpart in Birmingham are common sense elements. The Great Hall at Euston was a grandiloquent version of the most opulent 'stately home' and intended to reassure the upper orders and be uplifting for the middle classes and lower orders, as they could briefly benefit too. Rather than emphasise how many cubic yards of muck were moved or how many rails were needed, it is important to look at the broader picture. This allows us to the view the L&B in its own context.

This approach has relevance for the present too. In the 2020s, the HS2 rail link is progressing despite the controversy that surrounds it and claims that the money would be better spent on more modest improvements right across the rail network. What is amazing is that Hardwick's magnificent counterpart to Euston at Curzon Street station went out of passenger use by the 1850s. It survived as a dingy parcels and goods depot, but by the 1970s was almost derelict. Hardwick's building survived, unlike Euston, and will become the terminus building in Birmingham for HS2. In 1838, it was at the cutting edge of new transport technology. Before 200 years are up, it will be the grandiloquent terminus of the newest railway in Britain! Somehow, I think Glyn, Hardwick and Robert Stephenson would approve.

How do we explore what they achieved? I referred to Osborne's guide, which was illustrated with meticulous engravings of Euston and Curzon Street. This forms a wonderful contemporary record. The growth of traffic caused much of it to be swept away or downgraded in the nineteenth century, so the L&B of 1948 was heavily influenced by the London & North Western Railway from 1846 to 1923. That survived until electrification in the 1960s and the emergence of Britain's new railway. Steam vanished, as did Euston station, 4w goods wagons, mechanical signal boxes and many traditional station buildings.

It was my good fortune as a child to have a father who appreciated such things in so far as his workload as a GP allowed. After the age of five, and when school permitted, I explored it with him. However, when I was less than six months old, I was taken in my pram to see trains. We were near an SB, so I memorised and could repeat engine whistle codes and block bell codes used by signalmen. Indeed, I could indicate I was a fast train for the Beermingum before I could speak! Many railwaymen who dad knew were North Western, so there was a bias, as the LMS and BR were barely tolerated and the Midland an anathema.

I got to know the LNWR heritage, and although LNWR engines were few, SBs, signals and station buildings abounded. Much had disappeared by 1975, and memories are transient. Far more helpful is the photographic record that dad built up. With space for 158 views and 150 route miles, I have had to make a careful selection. As with previous books for Amberley, the illustrations are by some dedicated and talented photographers. First is dad, Dr Robert Preston Hendry (1912–91), who used his father's beautiful Rolleiflex 120, taking 12 2.25 in square negs, and moving to a Zeiss 35 mm camera in the 1960s, when I was learning on grandad's Rollei.

The earlier views are mostly by H. J. 'Jack' Stretton Ward. He was born in Coventry in 1895 but lived in Leamington. He developed an interest in trains, and from the age of fifteen, went on photo trips, at first accompanied by his mother, who sometimes appears in fashionable Edwardian apparel on a station seat. He used quarter plate glass negatives, so a dozen views were bulky and heavy. The camera had a low shutter speed, but when the subject was not moving fast, offered good views. Jack joined the Great Northern Railway engineers' office at King's Cross in 1912 and met Nigel Gresley. In 1914, he volunteered for the army but was turned down on health grounds. In 1915, he moved to Coventry as a test rider for the Premier Motor Cycle Co. and later Triumph, testing bikes in arduous conditions for dispatch riders on the Western Front. Apart from railways, his other love was bikes, so he was 'doing his bit' in a way he loved, but it ruined his health. Jack married in 1919, and became a motorcycle dealer, but the arduous test work left its mark. Jack died in 1958, and I later bought his negs.

The well-known and talented photographer Ray Tustin took his first photos in around 1936 and I bought his negs after his death and likewise the negatives of Pete Parish (1918–75), who also commenced filming in around 1935. A valuable perspective came from Tom Hayward, whose father had been a GWR driver. Tom worked as a draughtsman for the large BTH electrical engineering plant by the station and got to know the signalmen at all the Rugby boxes, as did dad.

The Osborne engravings are recognisably accurate, as with the Doric arch, and show the L&B on day one, so to speak. The need for enlargement meant much was swept away, and the 1960s high priests of the New Railway had no use for boring old rubbish, to our eternal loss, as their legacy is mundane.

Dad, Jack, Ray and Pete are the main contributors, but I know little about one other photographer. In dad's day, GPs visited sick patients. One patient called Mellish was a young married man, who took ill. Dad and he 'talked trains', and his widow spoke to dad about her husband having taken some railway slides and that he had told her to speak to 'the doctor' who would make sure she got a fair price for them. As we had bought several collections, we had an idea of what would be fair. Dad returned home one day with this slide collection. Two colour views at Willesden and two at Tring are included here to delight modern readers. Clive Partridge, a school classmate and lifelong friend who handled engineering access for West Coast route 'mod', has been invaluable, as has Mike Christensen.

A big debt goes to my wife Elena, brought up in the USSR, where railfans were uncommon. She has adapted to this peculiar English idea and joined me on film trips. I have spoken fondly about my parents indulging my passion for railways. As a kid, I would make models and show them to mum. She would praise them, but knew undeserved blanket praise is not good for a child, so it would be tempered with 'maybe next time, you can do even better'. A signal box diagram needed a lot of work. I had shown the improved version to Elena, and she praised it, but said it was a shame it was not better. After much effort, I was miffed but knew she was right. Two hours later, it was better, and I had learnt how to improve jpg files. The same skills have enhanced images selected for this book, so Elena has followed on in the role of mum.

I adopted this approach with our three girls, Anastasia, Amy and Katie, and the youngest corrected me sweetly one day. I said 'good lightning' had struck me three times with the three of them. Katie reproved me, pointing to mama and saying it was four times. How right she is!

This woodcut is from the 1875 LNWR official guide 'specially prepared for the use of American Tourists' and shows the Doric arch after 'EUSTON' had been inscribed on it in 1870. The view is from Euston Place to the courtyard beyond the arch and the station frontage.

'Royal Scot' class 460 No. 46120 *Royal Iniskilling Fusilier* of 1927 of Crewe North shed was rebuilt with a Stanier 2A taper boiler in 1944 and has arrived in platform 3 beneath the 1837 Stephenson train shed on an Up express in 1958. Platforms 3 and 4 were the same length, but platform 4 was shortened to allow the 'shanty' to the right of the engine.

When I was four, I was shown a saddle tank at Rugby shed with an immense chimney and told I would never see another. It had been designed by John Ramsbottom, Webb's predecessor at Crewe as Chief Mechanical Engineer from 1862 to 1871. The last place these 'Special Tanks' ran was as shunters at Wolverton carriage works. Ray Tustin took CD No. 7 outside the carriage works loco shed on 6 September 1953.

Near Wolverton (59¾ miles from Euston) the line crossed the valley of the River Great Ouse. Designed by Stevenson with six large elliptical central arches and three small flank arches at each end, the bridge was 659 ft long and 57 ft above river level. It was widened from double to quadruple track by the LNWR in 1879–82, and regarded as the greatest bridge on the L&B.

South of Rugby, Stephenson could go via the thriving town of Northampton, which was much lower lying than the surroundings, or via Kilsby. He opted for Kilsby claiming hostility from Northampton. When major problems arose with Kilsby, Stephenson adroitly laid the blame on Northampton. This is Kilsby Tunnel south portal, *c.* 1958. The high arch was to reassure passengers and the ornamental work atop the portal gives it a classical aura.

F. W. Webb handled signalling as well as engines and when contractors' equipment was unreliable switched to Crewe. The Rugby boxes dated from the rebuild of the station in the early 1880s. They were replaced in 1964 by a power box prior to electrification. Rugby No. 1 box, a nominal 180-lever capacity, was the largest size on the LNWR, but actually had one extra lever at the far end.

'Prince of Wales' 460 No. 25656 *Shark* had been LNWR 1084 and screams her Crewe design, as does the water column on the left, the fire 'devil' to stop it freezing in winter, the gas lamp and wooden bracket signal. The only obvious LMS presence is the 1930s concrete mechanical coaling plant.

Until the 1960s, Coventry proclaimed its LNWR ancestry. In 1910, Jack Stretton-Ward took 5 ft 6 in Webb 242T No. 897 on mixed fish, fruit and horsebox stock in the Up platform. The same engines were at work forty years later.

Hampton in Arden served a well-heeled area and received a new station with a medieval theme in 1884, with the entrance porch topped by an ecclesiastical quatrefoil window. This superb structure was torn down in favour of modern mediocrity during electrification.

Above: In LNWR days, Birmingham New Street had a magnificent train shed, but wartime damage resulted in it being replaced with simple canopies. 'Jubilee' 45681 *Aboukir* of Liverpool Edge Hill shed departs with an Up express. The loss of the train shed revealed how the station was surrounded by multistorey buildings. The lack of hard hats and HV jackets is typical of traditional post-war men.

Right: Robert Stephenson's memorial once appeared between the lodges at the entrance to Euston Road but is now located on the concourse of the rebuilt Euston. As his long-disused Curzon Street station in Birmingham will be the terminal for the new HS2 rail link, it is a fitting backdrop for his statue. Unlike most kings and politicians whose statues infest the land, despite the harm they do, Stephenson's legacy is one of doing good.

1

Euston, Camden and Willesden – The City Scene

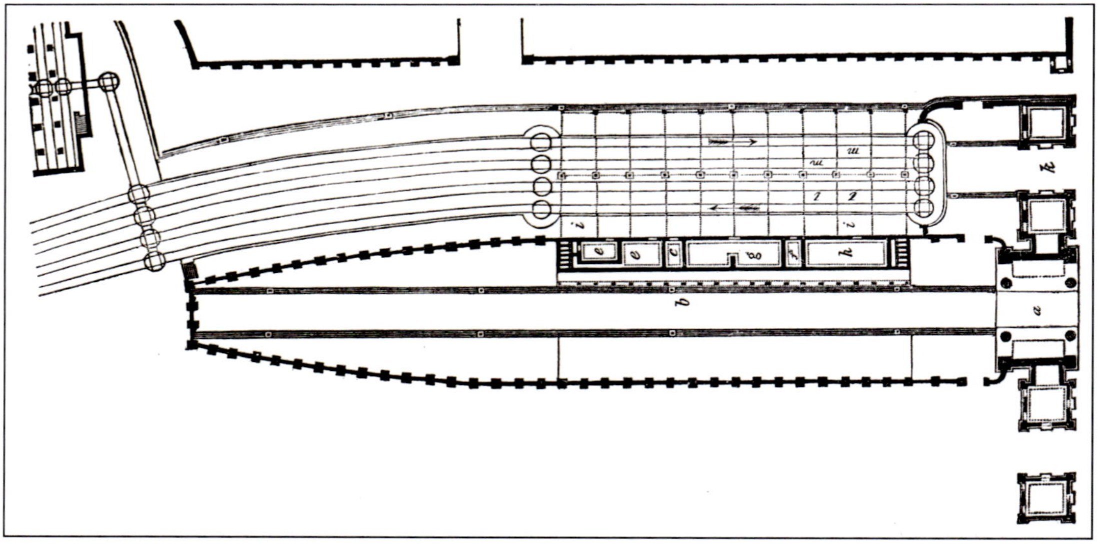

This 1838 plan of the Stephenson train shed at Euston makes an interesting comparison with the 1938 plan. It predates the Great Hall as just a narrow block of offices is shown next to the departure platform, but the curve is there for all time. 4w coaches were shunted via short wagon turntables.

Most views of Philip Hardwick's Doric arch in Yorkshire freestone from Bramley Fell quarries are from ground level, so it soars above us. It was not on Euston Road or Euston Square or Euston Street, but on the narrow Drummond Street, an area cleared in the remodelling of the 1960s. The Doric arch and the Great Hall divided the station in two, which to the 'old is bad' fanatics in the 1960s was fault enough. There were courtyards for taxis on either side of the arch, but the taxis dominate the scene.

I admired the arch, but I loved the Great Hall with its wonderful ceiling and ornate stairs to the boardroom of the LNWR, which I once had the privilege of visiting. It was 128 ft long, 62 ft wide and 64 ft high. The refreshment rooms off the Great Hall provided splendid food at a reasonable price. I recall one 'mere' waiter there who had the dignity and panache of a bishop or peer, and was probably far more useful than either.

Euston,
Jan., 1934.

I am glad to take this opportunity of sending New Year's greetings to all the L M S staff employed in Great Britain and Overseas, and to thank you all for your efforts during the period of depression through which we have been passing. He would be a bold man who would claim that we had reached the end of the trade depression; but there are unmistakable signs that, even if we have not turned the corner, the corner is in sight. There are, fortunately, definite indications of improvement in trade, this improvement being reflected in railway receipts, and since it can be truly said that railway prosperity is indicative of national prosperity, we are justified in looking forward to 1934 with high hopes of better times to come.

You will be aware, from announcements which have appeared in the press during the past year, of the many new developments which have taken place on the L M S. These developments are the result of careful study and research, and are not confined to one or two departments, but cover the activities of the whole organisation.

I believe every employee of the L M S is proud of the part our Company plays in the transport services of the country, and in order that you may be more easily brought into closer contact with the changes which are taking place throughout a system so wide and so diversified, I have arranged for a series of interesting articles describing some of the more important activities of the Company to be published monthly. In this issue is published the first of a series of articles which the Chief Commercial Manager will contribute monthly on current topics. There is also a message from the Head of the Claims Department.

In succeeding issues, some of the developments in mechanical appliances will be described, and each department will, from time to time, contribute items of interest.

J C Stamp

4

A few addresses achieve special status. Letters from the boardroom were headed with the company circular device, which was enough. They did not say LNWR or LMSR. This 1934 message from the chairman, Sir Josiah Stamp, to the staff followed tradition with the LMS seal replacing its LNWR predecessor. I visited the boardroom long before I was aware of the traditions, or that one day I would own a letter with the seal and nothing more that an address. If you didn't know what it meant, it was not for you!

Osborne's guide depicted the Stephenson train shed with its cast-iron columns and graceful arches connecting them. The train shed held four tracks, the outer two of which had raised platforms called parades. At first trains were hauled to Camden by a stationary engine and endless rope, but locomotive power soon took over.

In 1870, a new entrance drive was cut from the Doric arch to Euston Road, the entrance on Euston Road being flanked by rectangular lodges with the names of places reached from Euston carved into the prominent cornerstones. These were not the four lodge-type buildings of 1838 next to the Doric arch, three of which can be seen in the opening image of this chapter. Unlike the Drummond Street buildings, they survive.

To the east, the station was bounded by Seymour Street, later Eversholt Street. In 1933–34, a new headquarters for the LMS, Euston House, was built to the designs of architects A. V. Heal and W. H. Hamlyn, opening on 12 February 1934. It is no longer in railway use but is part of the Euston story.

Platform 3, as it became, was one of the original platforms to the east of the Great Hall, and Jack Stretton-Ward took a 'Whale Precursor' on a Birmingham express there in 1910. The roof is the original 1838 Stevenson roof, raised by 6 ft in 1870 with new decorative plinths added to increase the height. An early cab is on the cab road which ran the length of platform 2/3. The rotating backing out signals were an LNWR design.

In 1871–73, two extra platforms were added to the right of the original train shed with Seymour Street to the right. This photo, from a senior LMS loco officer called Spencer, who would have been present, shows the test run by the new Stanier 6200 *The Princess Royal* in August 1933 in platform 2. It is fitted with the prototype 4,000-gallon Stanier flat-sided tender No. 9000, and original pattern boiler.

Electric loco 87001 of 1973 became *Stephenson* in 1976, but was renamed *Royal Scot* in 1977, restoring a famous name to the West Coast Main line. No. 87001 is in platform 5, taken from platform 6 prior to sectorisation.

J. M. Dunn of the LNWR was shed master at Bangor in BR days. On 8 September 1930, he visited Euston and took LNWR Webb 062T coal tank No. 7748 on carriage pilot work in platform 1. A move to the Up carriage shed would be propelled by the train engine, but the Down carriage shed on the far side of Hampstead Road Bridge or facilities at Willesden had a lead engine and assistance from the train engine propelling, as they took the train via the underpass on the Down empty carriage line outside Euston.

A double-headed train with a 'Precursor' 440 and 'Prince of Wales' 460 is about to depart Euston shortly before 1914.

Stanier blue-livery 'Coronation' Pacific 6223 *Princess Alice* had only been commissioned on 28 June 1937 when Ray Tustin caught her entering platform 3 at Euston on the Up 'Coronation Scot' on 5 July 1937. The bridge in the background carried Ampthill Square No. 1 over the station throat, and was demolished during the 1960s rebuild of Euston.

On the far side of Euston, Ray Tustin stood on platform 14 as 'Princess' 6204 *Princess Louise* of Camden shed made a spirited start from platform 13 with a Down express on 20 August 1937 ready to pass beneath Ampthill Square No. 1 bridge. Note the banner signals secured to the bridge girders. She is carrying the 1936 sans serif block-style insignia and clashing low-mounted cab numeral.

No. 87006 of 1973 is ready to depart platform 12 at Euston on 25 June 1974 on an Anglo-Scottish service, the added power, compared with the class 86s, being for Shap and the like. My employers sent me to visit clients and the first priority in my briefcase was a 35 mm camera, hence this view!

Euston received a Westinghouse type L miniature lever frame in October 1952, the new box being on the north side of Hampstead Road bridge, replacing the existing Nos 1, 2 and 3 boxes. It was replaced by a panel power box on 25/27 September 1965. In this 1950s visit by our model railway team, dad stands with hands clasped behind his back.

Looking from the 1952 box a decade later, an English Electric type 4 crosses from the Up fast to the independent line to reach platform 1 on the Up Royal Scot. The line curving to the right of the box is the shunting neck for the Up carriage shed.

The 1957 DC 630v sets replaced the First World War LNWR Oerlikon stock, fifty-seven three-car sets being built. Two sets coupled together are on the Up DC lines and heading under Hampstead Road bridge at the throat of Euston station. The nearest coach, 61159, is a driving motor brake second, DMBS. They ran from Euston to Watford and on the Broad Street electrified services.

The first shed at Camden of 1837 was the hand-over point for rope haulage ex-Euston up Camden bank. The roundhouse was replaced by a straight shed but had to be supplemented by a larger depot further out at Willesden. Camden became the express passenger shed. J. M. Dunn photographed LNWR 'Experiment' 460 No. 5472 *Richard Moon* by the shed on 13 March 1933. The reign of these George Whale unsuperheated 460s was coming to a close, and it went later that year.

Looking from the 'short siding' at the 'country' end of the Up Fast at Willesden Junction (5½ miles), a double-headed express is in the Down main platform, the pilot engine being a graceful 'Lady of the Lake' 222, *c.* 1900. On the left are the Up slow platform, middle siding and Down slow. The LNWR used ringed arms on slow line signals at this time, one being above the tank engine in the middle siding.

Sadly, there have been periodic accidents on the L&B. Following a signalling error, two trains collided on the slow lines at Willesden Junction on 5 December 1910, the last two coaches of the leading train being badly telescoped, resulting in five fatalities.

The Webb 'coal tank' was a tank version of the 4-ft 3-in wheeled Webb 060 coal engines, but were mixed-traffic engines often used on local passenger trains, station pilots, etc. J. M. Dunn took coal tank 7792 at Willesden on 11 October 1930 with pre-1928 large numerals with the red/gold reversed corner LMS freight insignia.

As an LMS officer, Dunn was able to access places not open to the enthusiast. He photographed North London Railway 060T No. 7532 on 4 October 1930 on 'engine and brake van' duties near Willesden High Level Junction SB, where the NLR DC electric lines crossed over the LNWR tracks. Built at the NLR Bow works in 1879, she lasted until 1952.

Ray caught 6004, once LNWR 42 *Princess Louise*, and renowned as 'the last Claughton' at Willesden in 1939. She was rebuilt to 5X status with a large boiler in 1928 but lost her name to the Stanier 'Princesses' in 1935. She retained her LMS red livery with yellow and red lettering until withdrawal in 1949, but her celebrity status did not secure preservation and she was broken up at Crewe.

Ex-LNWR Whale 'Precursor' 440 No. 5243 had been LNWR 1642 *Lapwing* of 1906. J. M. Dunn caught her in Willesden shed yard on 29 February 1932. Behind her is the six-road carriage shed with no smoke outlets. On the right is the two-road coaling tower of 1920.

I mentioned a patient of dad's called Mellish, who died young, telling his wife to speak to 'the doctor' about his slides. This shot of 'Royal Scot' 460 No. 46146 *The Rifle Brigade* was taken at Willesden, after the last four engines at Camden were banished to Willesden on 9 September 1962, although 46146 had made the move in 1961.

Mellish's view of Britannia Pacific 70054 *Dornoch Firth* at Willesden on 18 August 1963 includes the concrete cenotaph elevated coaling unit. At the time, 70054 was a Crewe North engine, having started at Polmadie, and ended at Carlisle Kingmoor.

2

Stonebridge Park to Cheddington – Metropolis to Countryside

The LNWR did little to promote suburban traffic in the nineteenth century, but natural growth plus traffic to and from the North London Railway at Broad Street forced the construction of the new DC electrified lines after 1911. The new electric lines, which also served Euston, ran to Watford Junction. Electric services began in 1915. Motor Driving Coach 5741 of 1915 is at Stonebridge Park depot with the original three fixed louvres replaced by four louvres on doors in this photograph by J. M. Dunn on 1 November 1931.

Dunn photographed un-rebuilt 'Royal Scot' 6153 *The Royal Dragoon* pausing on the Up fast with a cup final special at Wembley station (8 miles) on 24 April 1948. It was a bonanza for BR as it was Manchester United vs Blackpool, with a 4-2 result, and a procession of long-distance extra trains. To the right are the slow lines and beyond that the goods yard.

The antique North London Railway four-wheelers said the cup final on 22 April 1932 had to have at least one London side. It was Newcastle vs Arsenal, 2-1 with a notorious Newcastle goal allowed by bad refereeing. The Arsenal fans who packed into these ancient coaches would angry, as a twelfth man on the other side is always a sore point.

A 'Britannia' approaches the forty-five-lever Harrow No. 1 box (11½ miles) with a freight on the Up slow. In the distance 36 signal for the Up slow is off and the slightly lower 38 for the crossover from the Up slow to the Up fast is at danger. The box is the later type 5 design, authorised in 1911 and opened *c.* 1915. On 8 October 1952, the signalman, per the timetable, crossed an Up local from the slow to the fast. Two minutes later a Perth–Euston express ignored the signals in patchy visibility and crashed into the local standing in the platform. A few seconds later, a northbound express ploughed into the wreckage, causing 112 fatalities.

The 1911 electrification required new DC tracks to parallel the fast and slow lines, as at Harrow No. 1. At Bushey & Oxhey station (16 miles), the electric lines curved away from the main line to loop through Watford and terminate at Watford Junction. Here the new lines and buildings at Bushey are seen looking south in April 1913.

Perhaps the most photographed water troughs on the LNWR were at Bushey. 'Precursor' tank No. 653 of 1906 heads a nine-coach evening local train on the Up slow to Euston, eight being six-wheelers. The lead vehicle is a fruit and milk van, as milk was then moved in churns.

Stephenson carried the L&B over the River Colne south of Watford by the 'five arches'. Like many of his bridges, it survives almost 200 years later, as he built for durability and strength, not to the lowest standard he could get away with. His caution must have saved the nation billions in repair costs.

The original Watford station was replaced in 1858 by Watford Junction and extensively rebuilt in 1909. Here the frontage of Watford Junction is seen with a 1911 LNWR Leyland thirty-four-seat open-top double-decker on the Watford–Croxley Green–Harrow route, abandoned in 1915 due to wartime problems, with two men peering under the bonnet seemingly investigating some issues. The station was rebuilt in 1984.

At Watford Junction, the shed was between the main line to Bletchley and the St Albans branch with the branch platform in the background. Dunn filmed 9072 a piano-front class G 080 on 6 September 1931. As LNWR 2569, it began in 1902 as a Webb class B four-cylinder compound with the piano front of these engines. Whale converted it to a class G simple in 1909, and it was upgraded to G1 in 1932.

A new three-road shed had been authorised near the Up slow platform in 1871 and soon doubled in size. 'Jubilee' 45606 *Falkland Islands* heads a Blackpool–Euston extra on 4 September 1949. The signal on the right with co-acting arms below the horizontal beam is unusual and controlled the Down slow to Down fast crossover.

Local opposition forced a poor choice of route on Stephenson near Watford, so he had to pierce high ground with a tunnel north of the station. He used a classical theme, as a Roman or Greek railway tunnel must be safe! When the slow lines were added, a second tunnel was bored, and the old bore became Watford West Tunnel. The modern overhead catenary does nothing for its looks, but the tunnel is substantially as created by Stephenson.

Berkhampstead (28 miles) was once a market town, but smallpox ended that. The engraving from Osborne of the 1838 station shows how modest the early stations were. It was replaced in 1875 about 300 ft away when the line was quadrupled. Proposals for a branch to Chesham and a narrow-gauge steam tramway failed.

Until the Beeching 'hatred' of summer Saturday trains to the seaside, rakes of elderly coaches were kept for peak summer weekends, as here. This Mellish shot of 70033 *Charles Dickens* of Willesden shed shows an extra near Tring on Saturday 18 August 1962 with Northchurch on the distant hill. Whether it was the GWR to Cornwall or the LNWR to Blackpool and North Wales, it was the same every weekend in the school holidays.

Mellish's photograph shows Riddles 9F No. 92120 of Leicester Midland shed no doubt having left the Midland line at Market Harborough for the LNW branch to Northampton and then via Roade to the main line on 18 August 1962.

There was a considerable lack of development at Cheddington, with just railwaymen's houses around. It was the junction for a LNWR branch to Aylesbury which came in on the left to an angled platform. The SB was at the north end of the station by the junction. For sighting reasons the Up fast platform starter, 3, is mounted on the same signal post as the Down slow home, No. 59.

3

Leighton Buzzard to Roade and Stow Hill

North of Leighton Buzzard station, No. 2 box controlled the junction to Dunstable from a seventy-lever Webb frame. In 1965, with the opening of Bletchley Power Box, it became Shunting Frame No. 2, to control the now freight-only Dunstable branch. Owing to the limited separation of the fast (far) and slow (near) lines, there was no room for a 12-ft base, so it was slightly oversailed on a narrower base.

About ½ mile north of Leighton Buzzard, Stephenson drove the double-track Linslade Tunnel, initially named Leighton Buzzard Tunnel, beneath Linslade woods. A single-track bore was added to the east and another one to the west in 1875, a medieval theme being applied to all three, as if Henry VIII had been a keen railway builder! The Osborne engraving, though overdramatic, captures the essentials evident today.

From early Victorian days to the close of the twentieth century, mail travelled by train and methods evolved of picking up and dropping mail bags at speed. Fourteen sets of apparatus existed between Euston and Crewe, with a net to collect mail bags and a hook to hold bags to be picked up, and similar apparatus on trains. Most mail trains ran in the night. Here an AM10 electric unit passes the apparatus near Leighton Buzzard on 24 September 1973.

Bletchley (46¾ miles) was so minor that it merited little comment in Osborne, but became an important junction with the east–west lines to Oxford and Cambridge. A modernist station in the 1960s stripped it of any architectural charm.

Bowen-Cooke's idea of a large-boilered 'Claughton' 460 was vetoed by the LNWR civil engineer, so it was only in LMS days that a large boiler was married to a 'Claughton' frame, some rebuilds additionally having Caprotti motion. The lack of a smokebox number plate means I cannot identify this Caprotti 'Claughton' on a Down express at Bletchley in 1932.

Bletchley shed was north of the station on the Down side, a trailing ladder of slips giving access to all running lines save Bedford, without a reversal. In the early 1930s, LNWR engines still ruled the roost, a rare exception being LMS 'Jinty' 7122. After the previous shed fell down in a gale, a new six-road shed was built in 1873. LNWR 440s and 460s handled passenger trains on both long branches.

The Bletchley breakdown train is in loco siding No. 2, as an English Electric type 4 powers by on the Up fast to Euston, *c.* 1962. The crane is RS1020, a 1909 LNWR Cowans Sheldon 25T crane. The top of Bletchley No. 2 box is visible above the first carriage. Bletchley No. 5 box, at an angle to the right of the type 4, was the first of over thirty boxes and crossing frames on the Cambridge branch.

Class AL3 No. E3098, of 1961, on a class 5 petroleum tanks train at Bletchley is in the original stylish electric blue with the rampant lion casting which was soon replaced. Not only is it a short-lived colour scheme, but colour print negs and prints were prone to fading.

At Denbigh Hall, a mile north of Bletchley, the L&B crossed the old Roman Watling Street, now the A5, on a skew bridge. Osborne cautioned, 'the traveller, on enquiring where is Denbigh Hall, has pointed out to him a mean looking beer shop situated by the side of the bridge.' When the navvies were building the L&B, an inn by the lineside was 'heaven' to them, and a fortune to the owner. The top of Denbigh Hall SB is in line with the engine in this view by Ray in April 1948.

Denbigh Hall gained further fame, as an inscription on the bridge reveals, 'Prior to September 1838, the southern part of this railway terminated at this bridge whence passengers were conveyed by coach to Rugby where they rejoined the railway for Birmingham. Inscribed by Sir Herbert Leon bart and Lady Leon of Bletchley Park, Bucks by permission of the L&NW Railway Company AD 1920.' Bletchley Park was the legendary home of the Second World War code breakers.

After Denbigh Hall, the line entered a shallow cutting with arch and span bridges at Loughton, just south of Wolverton.

Wolverton station, *c.* 1964. Osborne described Wolverton (52½ miles) as 'the grand central depot of the company ... an extensive establishment, and will probably give rise to the formation of a new town.... the engine house, which is 112 yards square ... upwards of fifty cottages belonging to the servants of the company ...'. Instead of becoming a locomotive depot, Wolverton became the carriage works of the LNWR.

Ray took a driving trailer car at Wolverton carriage works where the stock was towed by a steam loco for overhaul on 6 September 1953. Amongst the most comfortable and best riding stock of the day, the Oerlikon stock was far superior to its 1957 BR successors.

No. 6204 *Princess Louise* of 1935 heads the Up 'Royal Scot' towards Euston over Castlethorpe troughs, when headboards were tiny, as here.

By September 1964, the mechanical signalling at Roade had succumbed to Rugby Power Box and this scene looks north from the Down fast with the slow lines on the right, which will diverge to Northampton at Courteenhall bridge, the fast lines continuing via Kilsby to Rugby.

Blisworth station (63½ miles) served a small village, whilst Northampton, with 15,531 inhabitants, was 4 miles to the east. The construction of the 47-mile Blisworth–Northampton–Peterborough branch, with L&B backing, was authorised in 1843 and opened in 1845, dropping to low ground around Northampton. Webb 5-ft 6-in 242T No. 46666 of Northampton shed is on a Northampton motor in 1951.

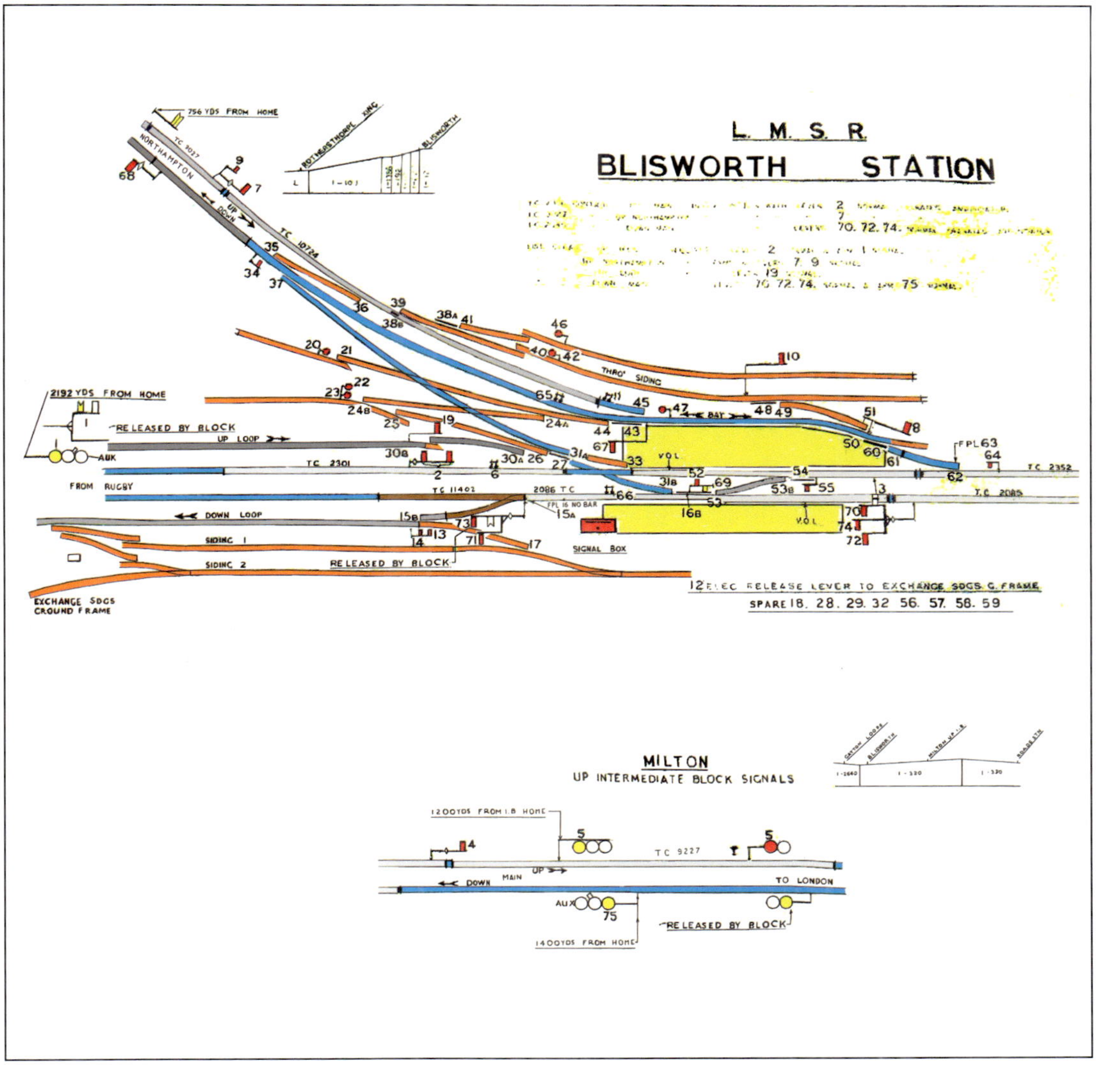

SB diagrams are in landscape format rather than in vertical portrait format, but most books appear in portrait format. A third of the width of Blisworth diagram shows the Up starter and the Milton IB, Intermediate Block, signal. For publication, I split it, allowing a 50 per cent increase in size on the page for the reader. The L&B branch to Northampton and Peterborough leads to the east. The Stratford-upon-Avon & Midland Junction line to Towcester ran from an adjacent station in the other direction, but was only reached via Exchange Sidings, and the LNWR box had no control over it. The LNWR seventy-five-lever Webb frame had eight spare levers in 1948. VOL refers to 'vehicle on line' indicators, which were an LNWR predecessor to electric track circuits to remind the signalman that a track was occupied. The diagram shows a drop at 1 in 103 from Blisworth to Rothersthorpe as Northampton was in a dip, and such grades were steeper than Stephenson desired.

Osborne says L&B comes to Banbury Lane Gates but this was before the Saxby & Farmer SB of 1878, which predated LNWR boxes. It had a S&F frame, replaced by a Webb frame in 1891. Although in the Rugby PSB area, it survived until 1988, as it worked the only level crossing between Euston and Coventry.

Stow Hill, now Stowe Hill, Tunnel was 500 yd long with an ornate portal. As this section was not quadrupled, Kilsby and Stow Hill tunnels have changed little since Stephenson's day. In Osborne's engraving, a 'policemen' gives an all-right signal to the driver of a train exiting the tunnel.

4

Weedon, The Kilsby Nightmare and Rugby

Above: Weedon was the junction for the single-track Daventry branch, extended in 1895 to join the Rugby–Leamington branch at Marton Junction. A new station was opened in 1888, when the heights of the running lines were altered to eliminate a movable bridge over a canal. It closed on 15 September 1958, when Daventry closed to passengers and was demolished. The station is seen here in the early 1900s.

Opposite above: Sir Richard Moon, the chairman of the LNWR, would spend freely if it was beneficial. In its 1885 Act, the LNWR gained authority for a 4-mile branch from Weedon to Daventry. As the main line crossed a branch canal into Weedon barracks just above canal height, a movable bridge carried the main line, so a new main line at a higher level replaced the old alignment. As with the Grand Union canal (see bridge through abutment), the main line was now well above Bridge Street, near Weedon.

Opposite below: At Three Bridges Road, Buckby Wharf, 86256 *Pebble Mill* in InterCity livery heads south with an Up express in September 1986. The nearest bridge is Stephenson's one from the 1830s and through the arch is the 1959 M1 bridge.

Welton was the last station before Rugby on the main line and was remodelled in 1891 with an SB on the Up platform replacing one further north. Midland compound 40923 double heads a Down express. At Welton, drivers of non-stop services gave a whistle code so the signalman could send a special train entering section code to Kilsby Tunnel South SB, which converted it to route code information for Kilsby North box and the Rugby boxes, so a 4 became a 4-4-4, 4-4-4-1 or 4-4-4-2 depending on the route.

Osborne's engraving of Kilsby Tunnel shows one track in the cutting and a fragile wooden prop in the 6 ft, so work is at an early stage. The lack of wing walls suggests it is the north portal, so the bridge carries Watling Street pro tem!

No. 46207 *Princess Arthur of Connaught* blasts out of the south portal of Kilsby Tunnel on carmine and cream stock on a Lime Street–Euston express, the engine being at Edge Hill shed from 1951 to 1959. This was the L&B at its best.

Taper boiler Royal Scot 46169 *The Boy Scout* exits Kilsby Tunnel North portal on a Euston–Manchester service on 6 August 1949, prior to receiving smoke deflectors.

Above: In the days when GPs did their 'rounds', which could be in double figures, six days a week, they knew their patch like a taxi driver, so we went to Norton Lane bridge north of Kilsby Tunnel in the 1970s. Under the computerised TOPS system, the AL6 class lost their E prefix, so E3140 became 86258.

Opposite above: The white roof domes of the original electric-blue livery showed up copper dust from the overhead, so were discarded. Full yellow ends appeared and BR arrows replaced the BTC 'lion and wheel' casting. E3146 heads 1A51, the 13.25 Liverpool (Lime Street) to Euston, which passed Rugby at 15.42 through Clifton Road Junction, south of Rugby. The old line via Kilsby and the new line rejoined here with a flyover to minimise conflicts.

Opposite below: The tracks at Rugby shed stopped short of the end wall, revealing the smoke troughs and the trusses supporting the roof. By the mid-1950s, the allocation had dropped from 160 locos to ninety and engine changing on expresses ceased, so the shed hosted 'Black Fives', 8Fs, LNWR 080s, Midland 2Fs and 4Fs, 262Ts and 264Ts. Here a couple of LNWR 080s, an Ivatt 262T and a 4F, are seen.

E3146
1A51

The 1934 LMS mechanical coaler at Rugby, with the GC 'birdcage' bridge in the distance, December 1961.

In 1964, I was revising for my GCE O levels, which distracted me from photography, but after I had sat the exams, I would say to mum, I might go 'Duchess' hunting and often struck lucky! One day, I found 46245 *City of London* light engine in Rugby, providing out-of-course activity in glorious weather.

Bowen-Cooke spent over twenty years in Rugby, and senior drivers in 1918 knew him well. With the 'Claughton' war memorial loco *Patriot* completed, they wanted it in Rugby for Remembrance Day 1919, and told the chief. When it was replaced by an LMS 5X, the younger men wanted that instead. The tradition included a line-up of veterans from both wars by the loco. No. 45500 *Patriot* was a 12A Carlisle Upperby engine from 11/54 to 8/58.

Rugby (82½ miles) was the most imposing station between London and Birmingham; seven lines radiated from it, four being main lines, with Peterborough not far short in status, so only two were 'branch lines'. Engines on the Up and Down Irish Mails changed at Rugby, and after using 440s in the early 1900s, the Up and Down pilots became 460s. The engine on the right is in the Down pilot siding, and to the left are the Leamington and Leicester bays. The main glory is the train shed roof and the superb lamps.

Pete Parish filmed a spotter watching as crimson lake 46243 *City of Lancaster* on a 'non-stop' Up express took water. Alos seen are the column for the LNWR train shed, an LMS bracket signal, an LNWR water column, the LMS mechanical coaling plant and a 1939 colour light signal.

48657 and 45027 are coupled together to move along the Up and Down engine line at Rugby during the 'Big Freeze', 10 February 1963. They are between the train shed and the up carriage shed and are signalled to the Up running lines.

As LMS 800hp Bo-Bo No. 10800 was withdrawn by 1963, this photograph dates from earlier than that. This highly unreliable engine departs from the Up platform on an express, but with colour lights, and it is not possible to determine the route from the 'wrong' direction. It is surprising it should have been let loose in such weather, as photos hauling trains are rare. With Gresley carriages, Peterborough seemed likely, and if it failed it was not a key route. Later, I found it had a Peterborough turn, so the deductions were spot on.

Another lovely view of brand-new class AL6 No. E3149, which was completed at the Vulcan Foundry works at Newton-le-Willows in April 1966 and came to Rugby for an exhibition in the former Leicester bays at the station. As dad knew the BR folks, I was asked into the cab and allowed to drop and raise 'the Pan', or overhead collector. It became TOPS class 86.

Rugby No. 4 box was off the Down platform and save for a bolt lock to permit Up/Down shunts, did not signal the Up. It worked connections to the Down yard and was a type 4 box from the 1880s rebuild of the station with a ninety-lever Webb frame.

No. 4 box was involved in the legendary fireman blockage of the WCML. A fire at the BTH was tackled from Railway Terrace, so the hoses had to run from the street hydrants across all Up and Down lines. A fireman, Tom Hayward, who knew the boxes and the men, had to explain how the fire service had the right to do so with a fire. It was an incident worthy of the *Titfield Thunderbolt* film!

The 1838 passenger station at Rugby was on the Birmingham side (left) of Newbold Road bridge at Rugby. The bridge was castellated in Gothic style with a four-centred arch. Leading architect A. W. Pugin was contemptuous, saying because Rugby School used such architecture, the L&B copied it. The bridge was widened on both sides for the Trent Valley and Leamington lines, which diverge a few yards to the west. The pedestrian arch on the right survives.

Above: George Whale converted many Webb 080s to simples. A class C1 080 simple is signalled by No. 7 box from the Up Trent Valley to Up Goods Loop No. 1, *c*. 1910. The switch diamond marks the divergence of the Birmingham and Trent lines. The right-hand line at the bottom of the photo is the Up Birmingham, and the left-hand line, the Down Trent. It is astonishing that fifteen-year-old Jack was allowed to stand here!

Left: Pete Parish, from my father's model railway team, had excellent contacts with BR and was given even better access in the early 1950s. The SB is the replacement LMS Rugby No. 7, as the LNWR box was on the embankment on the left and gradually sliding down the slope due to clay soils.

The only intermediate station between Rugby and Coventry was featured in my book *Rails Aound Rugby*, so Stafford's 2P No. 40646 on one of Cam Camwell's SLS Specials approaches from Birmingham with the new 1960s BR flyover which was to replace the level junction to the right on 14 April 1962. The engine was gleaming, though it was to be withdrawn on 12 May. A delightful guy, Cam is missed by all who knew him.

The Rugby shedmaster had a tale to tell. In 1964, locos that might be close to the danger flash zone of the 25 kV had to be notified to HQ, so he added 49078 to his list, as it had been stored at Rugby since before the 'Big Freeze' of 1963. He was told to correct his list, as it had been scrapped. My innocent sixteen-year-old's request of 'well let's keep it then' was alas not on, so we had to convince HQ that we did have an LNWR 'Super-D', which was the last LNWR loco on the London & Birmingham. So, in July 1964, the last of the last departed.

5

Northampton and the Perennial 'New Line'

Above: The 1845 line from Blisworth dropped steeply to Northampton (Bridge Street), so was unsuited as a main line, although it sometimes saw main line trains. There were block posts at Rothersthorpe Crossing, Duston Sidings and Duston West (junction), where the low-level line split to the old Bridge Street or for Rugby.

Opposite: The new route had to enter Northampton higher than the Blisworth line and crossed the old line at right angles on a girder bridge. A new SB, Duston West, controlled both lines from two lever frames in the box at right angles. It had to be of extraordinary height, so the operating floor was above the high-level tracks. The low-level frame received trains from the Blisworth direction and offered them to Castle station via Duston North or to Bridge Street.

In this view of Duston West, we are on the Blisworth side of the box on the low level and see the stairs to the operating floor and the door to the locking room at mid-level.

DUSTON WEST

Above: The high level was simpler, with just a trailing crossover on the Roade side of the box. The operating floor, though high for the low level, was low for the high level. The type 4 is on an Up Northampton–Roade service, *c*. 1962.

Opposite above: Trains on the Roade (high level) line ran from Duston West (high-level frame) to the all-timber fifty-nine-lever Northampton No. 1 box, at the south end of Northampton Castle station, seen on 6 December 1970. The tracks in shade by the box are to Duston North Junction and then to the 1845 Bridge Street station or Duston West Junction, low-level frame. Behind the box are the old platforms 4 and 5.

Opposite below: The 1859 station at Northampton Castle was too modest for its new role, so a classical new station opened in 1881, seen in 1957. The main buildings were on the Up No. 1 platform serving the Up slow, and the Up main line beyond it, but without a platform face. In the distance is West Bridge. The buildings were replaced by a modernist structure in 1966.

Northampton
← 150 yards

Riddles 9F No. 92110 heads a class 7 unfitted freight, limited to 40 mph, on the Up main. The LMR 'running in board' should be a model for modern designers with their lower-case efforts, but common sense is uncommon with modern designers.

Northampton remained an oasis of mechanical signalling long after Rugby PSB was commissioned in 1964. It also retained a complex layout as in this April 1970 view of the 118-lever LNWR type 4 No. 2 box.

The eighty-four-lever Northampton No. 4 box was north of the station next to the Up slow before the divergence of the 1880s 'New Line' to Rugby and the older 1850s Northampton & Harborough line, which joined the LNWR Rugby–Peterborough line at Market Harborough and the Midland Leicester/Derby main line. Mechanical signalling at Northampton fell to Rugby PSB on 28 July 1991.

Local stations existed between Northampton and Rugby on the New Line, the last being Long Buckby, although the LNWR buildings have now gone. The line crossed the road on a bridge, so the booking office and forecourt were at road level with stairs to the platforms. Here the LNWR booking office is seen on 29 July 1971.

The platform buildings were timber with a ridge and furrow roof and matching canopy when opened on 1 December 1881. As the station is 4 miles from Daventry, which lost its rail services in the 1950s, it acts as a 'park & ride' for the town. This view looks towards Northampton on 29 July 1971. Note the excellent maroon/cream running-in board on the Up platform. Modern mediocrity and a ticket machine now suffice.

In the 1950s, dad wanted to model an LNWR station accessed from a road bridge and steps down to the tracks, i.e. the opposite to Long Buckby. Kilsby & Crick station was ideal. During measurements, 46249 *City of Sheffield* thundered past on the Down 'Royal Scot' on a weekend diversion.

The platform buildings were similar to Long Buckby with a ridge and furrow roof and matching cantilevered canopy. It avoided supports in the platform but put severe strains on the building, so was cut back.

The main objective of dad's visit was the two-storey booking office, with access at road level, and covered footways/stairs to the platforms. Due to limited space, dad could not get the entire building in the viewfinder, but so meticulous is his model that it gives a better than real portrait. It survives on the model railway he started in 1921.

A comic song from the 1950s proclaimed 'the railroad runs through the middle of the house', and at Clifton Road Junction at Rugby, where the New Line rejoined the old line, the Down Northampton ran through the middle of the SB on a flyover to avoid conflict with the Up London. The engine is LNWR 1997, a Whale 19-in goods 460, which was a freight version of his 'Experiment' passenger 460s.

6

Coventry, Edward Bury and Ecclesiastical Hampton

The only intermediate station between Rugby and Coventry was Brandon & Wolston (see my book *Rails Around Rugby*). Beyond Brandon, the L&B crossed the River Sow on an unusual viaduct of six small arches and a central large one with a 60-ft span. It was 52 ft high and almost 300 ft long.

Above: Coventry station (94 miles) was where the line was crossed by a road from Coventry to Kenilworth and Warwick. The booking office fronted the road and passengers descended by steps to the ground-level platform as per Osborne's engraving where a Bury 220 enters the station. Anyone familiar with the pre-1960 station would find it hard to reconcile the two, but the next photograph helps.

Opposite above: The original booking office was on Warwick Road next to Stephenson's 1838 bridge. Looking from a DMU in 1956, Jack photographed that historic bridge, which was destroyed in the station 'upgrade'. Through the arch is the Up platform and canopy of the 1840 station.

Opposite below: Having located the bridge, this view from the other side of Warwick Road bridge is a goldmine. The arch is seen, looking towards Birmingham. To the left is the 1838 London & Birmingham Railway engine shed and, in front of it, an Edward Bury water column. Between the LNWR platform starter and the water column is the Saxby & Farmer Coventry No. 2 SB dating from the 1870s. To the right, parcels stock obscures the 1838 station at ground level. The twin-gabled roof with chimneys on Warwick Road is Stephenson's 1838 passenger station, used for staff purposes.

Above: This view is in the opposite direction, towards Rugby, passing over the points to the L&B loco shed. It depicts both 1840 platforms, the luggage and passenger footbridges and the long building on the Up side that replaced the Stevenson station on Warwick Road.

Opposite above: Webb 5-ft 6-in 242T No. 1148 is on the Up main at Coventry in 1910. Jack had seen them in 1910 and forty years later they would still be on the same duties. They were pointed out to me as 'proper' engines, i.e. LNWR.

Opposite below: Bulleid Southern diesel 10201, which had come to the LM region, enters Coventry Up platform on an express in the early 1950s. I have usually moved from Euston TO Birmingham in each section, but Coventry's first station was at the road bridge and the 1840 station nearer Euston, so presenting the story as it happened seemed better.

Ribbons
Carbon

Ramsbottom DX goods 3184 drifts tender first along the Down main with an LNWR freight brake in 1910. The fireman is on top of the tender for better visibility, his mate staying at the regulator.

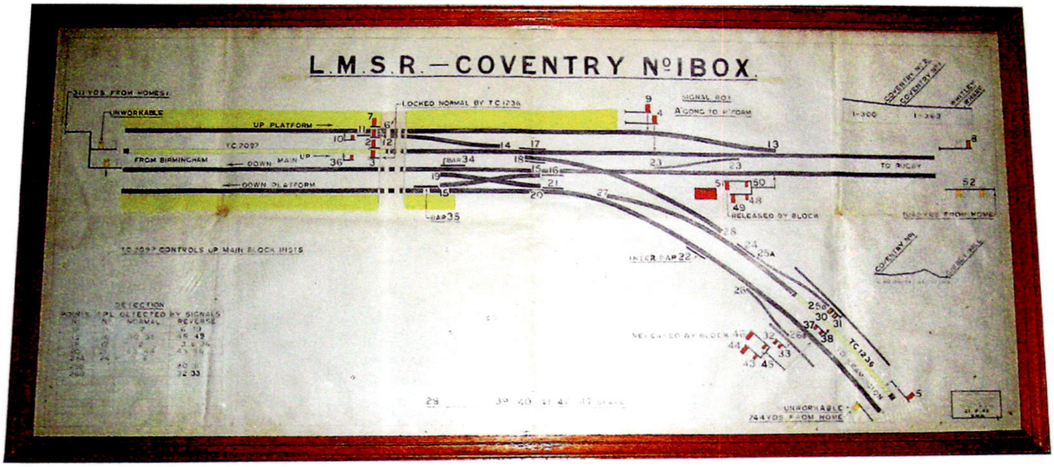

The LNWR type 4 Coventry No. 1 box worked the divergence of the Leamington and London lines at the east of the station and connections to the loco shed off the Leamington line using levers 1–52 and gong lever A to the platform. The view of SR diesel 10201 in the Up platform showed the four under-hung signals from the overbridge, 7, 11, 2 and 3. The two shunt signals in the six foot, 10 and 36, are LNWR square, 90-degree, rotating face ground signals.

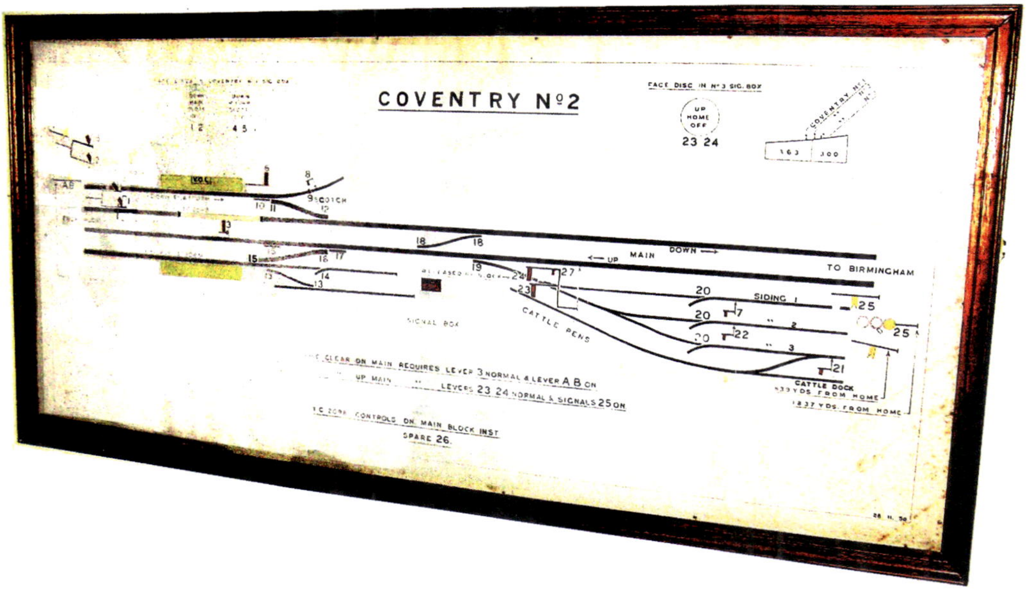

Coventry No. 2 diagram suffered from bad reflections if shot 'square'. The box, with twenty-seven numbered levers and A/B, is seen in the view of the Edward Bury 1838 water crane. It was a Saxby & Farmer type 2 box of 1874, predating LNWR boxes, but received a Webb frame in 1887. The short lead off the Down platform is to the L&B loco shed, which uses a scotch block, No. 9, instead of a trap. It can be seen in the view of the Bury water column as a triangular dark block above the rail.

The destruction of the old station building for the new BR station prompted BR to erect a wooden chalet in the car park suitably inscribed temporary, lest people assumed it was the station to be!

The demolition of the luggage bridge between the platforms was solved by an LMS BG and 262T No. 40104, which shuttled between the platforms with luggage. Dad and I were taken for a trip, but whether this was routine or because the enginemen knew him is unknown.

In an early Pete Parish view from *c.* 1935, *Engineer Watford* pays one of its last visits to Coventry, as it went in 1936, as the last active LNWR 240. It was one of the 'small jumbo' 6 ft 0 in 'Whitworth' or 'Waterloo' series and had been No. 793 *Martin*. It received a capital stock number in 1923 but became *Engineer Watford*. The 'Engineer' plates were 36 in long!

The 1838 loco shed on a facing lead off the Down platform could at most hold a couple of engines, with no room for expansion. In 1866, a small two-road LNWR loco shed was built in the divergence of the Leamington and Rugby lines, enlarged to four roads in 1897. With a peak of twenty, mostly freight engines, it was a minor sub-shed of Rugby and closed in 1958. Jack photographed it in 1910.

Crossing gates existed at Canley from 1838, and passengers could board trains from *c.* 1850, but it was trivial. The creation of a large Standard Motor Co. works by the station prompted a rethink and Canley Gates halt opened on 13 September 1940. The photo shows the oil lamps on the platform ready for lighting at dusk and the rudimentary station building. It was replaced by BR with a massive structure and the notorious Canley Gates level crossing abolished, so motorists had to use other roads.

Above: The theme of the Coventry section was the miraculous survival of 1838 L&B buildings until the desecration from 1959. Tile Hill, a tiny wayside station on the outskirts of Coventry, had its original track-level booking office between road and rail. It was old fashioned so had to go, eliminating another precious survivor from the dawn of railways. Dad photographed it during its demise on 19 March 1966.

Opposite above: The L&B track-level booking office with a raised platform beyond the level crossing and an LNWR type 4 oversailed SB this side of the crossing. Although Coventry PSB was to take over on 2–4 July 1966, crossing boxes were to be retained, but the LNWR box was replaced with a LM Region type 15 box on the opposite side of the level crossing. It took over from the LNWR box on 4 July 1966, being replaced by CCTV in July 1979.

Opposite below: Several cuttings existed west of Coventry, culminating in Beechwood Tunnel and cutting needing removal of 193,766 cubic yards of material by hand. The tunnel had an Egyptian motif, as the pharaohs would obviously be good railway builders! A single-arch bridge with a 76-ft span, 'springing from the naked rock', i.e. without abutments, was near one tunnel mouth. The stone for the arch came from the cutting itself.

Above: Berkswell, 19 March 1966. The station had altered little since LNWR days with a nineteenth-century wooden building, oil lamps, a wooden platform and LNWR level crossing and box, all of which were destroyed over the next few years. After one level crossing in the 82 miles from Euston to Rugby, there were four in a few miles.

Opposite above: Hampton-in-Arden was described by Osborne as a picturesque village. The original Hampton station became junction for the Birmingham & Derby Junction line within months, but this soon lost importance. In 1884, a new station, Hampton-in-Arden, ¼ mile to the south-east, opened on the LNWR. This is the SB, with a twenty-two-lever frame, on 19 March 1966.

Opposite below: LMS/MR compound 41122 had been a Monument Lane engine for part of 1949, but moved to Rugby for the next decade, so would handle Rugby–Birmingham local services at both sheds.

HAMPTON IN ARDEN

7

'Beermingum' – The Second City

The small communities near Coventry looked to that city, whilst villages closer to Birmingham were orientated to 'Brum'. Marston Green was a level crossing box at a wayside station, with a thirty-lever frame on the Up side, so the view is towards Birmingham. It was close to what was then Elmdon Airport, and in the event of an aircraft crashing, emergency colour light signals could be activated on the Down side.

The construction of the National Exhibition Centre beside the line included a new station, which would also be closer to Birmingham International Airport than Marston Green. The NEC starts with the dark area on the left. It is that close! The architect was Ray Moorcroft and International, which opened on 26 January 1976, is seen here on 2 July 1976.

I have criticised the tasteless modernism of Euston, Northampton, Coventry and New Street, as if the designers knew they were making a good job bad. International is the exception, with clean lines and a spacious interior. It is a short walk along the covered way to the NEC; a MAGLEV, on an elevated 'track', connected the station and airport from 1984 to 1995. When it wore out, parts were unavailable, so a Doppelmayer cable car system replaced it in 2003.

This is the surviving architectural gem of the L&B. The initial ideas of the L&B and Grand Junction railways were an end-on through station, but opposition made two side-by-side termini inevitable. The architect, Philip Hardwick (1792–1870), designed the Doric arch at Euston, but created an Ionic Revivalist frontage to Curzon Street. Services to Rugby began on 24 June 1838, but Kilsby delayed full opening until 17 September 1838.

Two parallel wrought-iron train sheds projected behind the Hardwick building, covering six tracks and two platforms. They were 217 ft long × 113 ft wide. With other railways entering Birmingham, this terminal became inconvenient and was replaced by New Street in 1854. It was put to freight and parcels use for over a century.

Curzon Street yard with the Hardwick building left of centre, July 1976. The hotel block of 1841, to the right of the original Hardwick building, still survived. The hotel closed in 1900, becoming railway goods offices. Freight use continued from 1854 to 1966 after which it was primarily used by Parcelforce.

The awkward terminal at Curzon Street prompted the LNWR to open a new through station in 1852. The crescent truss roof was by E. A. Cowper and with a 212-ft span and 840-ft length was then the biggest in the world. The pedestrian footbridge was, inconveniently, a public right of way. Wartime bomb damage to the North Western roof prompted its early removal.

Cowper's magnificent truss roof is seen here, as is the 1885 Midland Railway extension of the station. Improbably, Queen Street runs the length of the station dropping to platform level to avoid the footbridge and climbing again. The 3-ft 6-in gauge blue and ivory tramcars of Birmingham Corporation served the city until 1953, with half a dozen seen here.

Webb 6-ft 6-in 'Precedent' No. 5000 *Princess Beatrice* of 1875 has express passenger headlamps, or station pilot lamps, as mail is loaded on platform 4. Assuming her LMS identity in 1928, Jack photographed her at New Street in May 1929. The 'pagoda' on stilts above the footbridge is the shelter for the No. 5 signalman and his block instruments, but the levers were in the open, under the train shed roof!

Pete took coal tank 58900 in the four-track section between platforms 3 and 4 after the 1947 removal of the Cowper train shed, looking north from platform 4. Rather than an express code, it is likely to be a pilot engine code with one red and one white lamp, but you cannot be sure with black and white views.

Pete filmed from platform 4 as Bulleid diesel No. 10203 left platform 3, with an Up express for Euston. The sixty-lever New Street No. 1 box is to the right of the cavernous Worcester Street bridge, which carries properties as well as the road. Beyond the bridge is the tunnel mouth. The box was so busy that although it was usually only 100-lever boxes that had two signalmen, this box had two.

Looking from platform 4 towards Wolverhampton as AM10, later class 310 unit 063, enters New Street station in 1976.

Bescot was parent 3A depot under the LMS but was near Walsall, so remote from Birmingham. Of the nearby sheds, Aston was in the V of the Grand Junction to Curzon Street/New Street and the Stechford cutoff. It had a twelve-road Webb Northlight shed and a peak of fifty to sixty engines. This included Watford tanks in LNW and LMS days which were a large-wheeled passenger version of the coal tank. No. 6921 in seen 1931 in pre-1928 livery.

Freight work predominated and in 1931 Webb 'Cauliflower' goods, so named due to the LNWR 'crest' on the splasher, were plentiful. No. 8551 dated from 1900 and ran until 1949.

The other 'local' shed was Monument Lane, with a mix of passenger tanks, shunters, including 'Jinty' 16450, freight engines and some passenger engines.

From New Street station, the Wolverhampton line ran west, the first station being Monument Lane separated from New Street by two tunnels, the second of which was yards from Monument Lane shed, which is on the right in Jack's 1931 study. He included the far portal of the tunnel in his view. The factory above the tunnel mouth emphasises the busy and crowded nature of the West Midlands.

Introduction

Welcome to *Northern Diesels: DMUs in the North of England.* The following pages highlight the different types of DMUs that have operated and that have been seen in the North of England from the British Rail era in the late 1970s to privatisation and through to the present day at varied locations and on various workings. The geographical spread is northwards from Staffordshire to Cumbria, taking in Cheshire, Crewe, Manchester, Merseyside, Lancashire and northwards to Carlisle, while also covering the Tyne, the Tees, Yorkshire, including the York, Leeds, Bradford, Doncaster and Sheffield areas, as well as North Lincolnshire.

This book is intended to be a companion volume to my previous book – *Northern Electrics: EMUs in the North of England.*

What is a DMU? A Diesel Multiple Unit usually consists of one or more coaches with driving cabs at their outer ends. DMUs have at least one powered coach (car) and can operate with a powered or non-powered trailer car that has a driving cab, whilst others can be formed with powered or unpowered intermediate trailer cars coupled between the driving cars. Many present-day DMUs have powered cars throughout. The majority of Diesel Multiple Units have the engines located below the floor, although some examples (mainly on the Southern Region of BR) had their engines located above the floor in a dedicated area, but with reduced passenger-carrying capacity. Throughout the years, DMUs have had various types of transmission which converts the power of the diesel engines to move the train:

- Mechanical transmission, where the train is powered via a clutch, gearbox and final drive.
- Electric transmission, where the diesel engine(s) provides power to traction motors, which generate electricity to power the unit.
- Hydraulic transmission, providing power using oil through a torque converter and a gearbox/final drive to move the train.

The principle advantages of a Diesel Multiple Unit versus a locomotive-hauled train are:

1. All coaches (cars) are passenger carrying.
2. Easier and quicker turn rounds at terminal stations.
3. Cheaper to operate than an individual locomotive and carriages.
4. Lighter weight, reducing wear on the railway infrastructure and giving economical fuel consumption.
5. Easier maintenance and cleaning.
6. Units with sliding passenger entrance/exit doors reduce dwell time at stations.

Many recent designs/conversions are hybrids, where diesel engines are fitted to what is essentially an Electric Multiple Unit to increase operational flexibility on non-electrified routes (Classes 769, 800/1, 802/2, 802/3 and 805).

In the 1920s and 1930s all of the big four railway companies, GWR, LNER, LMS and SR, had experimented with diesel railcars or multiple units, but it was Great Western Railway, with their

Running on diesel power, Northern Flex Class 769 No. 769424 was departing from Parbold with the 15.17 Southport to Alderley Edge service on 12 March 2022. Northern has eight operational 769s that were converted from Class 319 EMU's by Brush Traction in 2017/18. Whilst retaining their pantograph for use on 25kV electrified lines, the units each have a pair underfloor MAN D2876 520-hp turbo-diesel engines.

fleet of thirty-eight diesel railcars that were built between 1934 and 1942, that were the genesis of the Diesel Multiple Unit (DMU) on Britain's railway network. Numbered 1–38, numbers 1 to 34 were all single units with driving cab at each end, but with an eye to the future, cars 35 to 38 were single-ended with a cab at one end, enabling two of them to work back to back to form a multiple unit and, if necessary, work with an intermediate passenger coach inserted between the two cars to increase passenger-carrying capacity as required, creating the format and style of Diesel Multiple Units for the future.

Post-Second World War, and following the nationalisation of Britain's railways in January 1948, with an eye to reducing costs and replacing steam-hauled push-pull, suburban and local stopping services, BR introduced newly built Diesel Multiple Units (nonstandard Derby Lightweight and Metropolitan Cammell designs) in specific areas: Cumberland, East Anglia, East Lancashire and West Yorkshire between 1954 and 1956.

The British Railways Modernisation Plan that was announced in 1955 would eventually see some 4,600 individual DMU cars ordered of various types and designs, built at the BR workshops at Derby, Eastleigh and Swindon, as well as a plethora of private companies – Birmingham Railway Carriage & Wagon (BRCW), Cravens Ltd, Gloucester Railway Carriage & Wagon (GRCW), Metropolitan Cammell, Park Royal, Pressed Steel & Wickham. Known as the First Generation DMUs, most of the fleet was long-lived and the final examples (Metropolitan Cammell Class 101s) were not withdrawn from regular timetabled passenger-carrying service in the North until 2003. Many of the designs underwent minor refurbishment in the mid-1970s, but with most rolling stock having a fatigue life of around forty years, by the early 1980s it was becoming clear that wholesale replacement of the BR Diesel Multiple Unit fleet was becoming a priority. Cost considerations saw the introduction of the infamous Pacer railbus fleet

GWR Diesel Railcar No. 4 was stored in the warehouse at the National Railway Museum at York on 24 November 2024. The streamlined vehicle had been introduced in 1934, with an AEC chassis and engine, and bodywork built by Park Royal with forty-four seats.

The Derby Lightweight DMUs were the first BR production DMU vehicles and were introduced from 1954. In later years, the small fleet was deemed as nonstandard and all were withdrawn from passenger use in 1969. One two-car unit survived as the Ultrasonic Test Train formed of cars DB975008 (ex-DTCL M79612) and DB975007 (ex-DMBS M79018) and was stabled in the sidings at Dock Street, Preston, on 7 May 1983. The unit was replaced by a Class 101 in 1986, and the last surviving two-car Derby Lightweight, seen here, passed into preservation.

(Classes 141, 142, 143 and 144) between 1984 and 1987, which heralded the first of the Second Generation DMUs, which eventually included Classes 150, 153, 155, 156, 158, 159, 165 and 166. Most of these fleets are now over thirty years old, and are still the mainstay of many local, regional and some longer-distance services across the UK railway network. The privatisation of BR in the late 1990s saw the introduction of various designs, which included Classes 168, 170, 171, 172, 175, 180, 185, 195, 197, 220, 221, 222 and 230, some of which date from the twenty-first century, and are still relatively new.

In one form or another and with a multitude of designs, the humble and unglamourous Diesel Multiple Unit has been the Cinderella of the UK railway network for over sixty years, and whilst they have ensured the survival of many routes and services that they have operated, what does the future hold for these unsung workhorses? Whilst electrification would be desirable for the entirety of the national network, the cost and practicality will limit any future electrification schemes, and despite the push to net zero the Diesel Multiple Unit still has a role to play for the time being, with modern clean and low-emission engines, hybrids, hydrogen power and the use of bio fuels ensuring their continued operation and survival for many years to come.

The following pages highlight a variety of DMUs, new and old, going about their daily business. The images show a selection of liveries, pre- and post-privatisation, many of which are now history. I have tried to give a varied selection of locations, with some getting a little more coverage to showcase a variety of types in service. The images may inspire some to get out and about to travel on, and to record what is still in service – in a rapidly changing system, the daily routine becomes history sooner than you think!

Finally, thank you to the team at Amberley Publishing for their assistance and as always thanks to my wife, Gillian.

Martyn Hilbert
Preston, Lancashire

East Midlands Railway Class 170/5 Turbostar No. 175510 was arriving at Blythe Bridge with the 84 Mile, 15.10 Crewe to Newark Castle service (1N19) on 9 March 2024. Derived from the Class 165/166 Networker Turbos, EMR operates the largest fleet of Derby-built Class 170s.

On a damp 29 June 1985, a Derby Etches Park-allocated (EP522) Swindon *Cross-Country* Class 120 DMU, with Driving Motor Second Lavatory car (DMSL) M53678 leading, was stabled between duties in the bay platform on the east side of Stafford station alongside Railway Street. Built at Swindon Works between 1958 and 1961, 194 individual cars were built, formed into three-car sets. In their construction, Swindon utilised the jigs that had been used for the later batches of GWR railcars.

Leaning into the curve, Avanti West Coast Class 221 Voyager No. 221116 was passing Heamies Bridge on the northern approach to Norton Bridge whilst working the 08.52 Edinburgh Waverley to London Euston service (9M52) on 18 May 2022. The Avanti fleet of Voyagers were withdrawn from service in December 2024, being replaced by Hitachi-built Class 805/807 units.

In a scene that has now passed into history, running nose to nose, sister Class 221 Voyagers Nos 221108 and 221107 were hurrying southbound at Chorlton with the 09.20 Chester to London Euston service (1A19) on 16 August 2023. The fleet of Class 221s was originally ordered by Virgin Trains and entered service in 2002.

In its Heart of Wales orange livery, Wales & Borders Class 153 No. 153320 was departing from Crewe with the 14.47 service to Shrewsbury on 9 August 2003. The short-lived Wales & Borders franchise ran from October 2001 to December 2003 when its operations were transferred to Arriva Trains Wales. No. 153320 is now one of twenty-four 153s operating for Transport for Wales (TfW), based at Cardiff Canton Depot.

In its bright 'Robin Hood Line 1993–2003' livery, Central Trains Class 170/5 Turbostar No. 170513 was arriving at Crewe with a Birmingham New Street to Liverpool Lime Street service on 31 July 2004.

A two-car Park Royal Class 103 DMU was coupled to a Class 108, at Crewe with a service to Chester on 19 May 1981. There were twenty two-car Park Royal Class 103 sets built at the Crossley Motors works in Stockport in 1957. The leading car seen here was Driving Trailer Composite Lavatory (DTCL) M56155, complete with its first-class saloon with orange curtains. The last of the Park Royals were withdrawn in 1983. The bay platform in this view is now out of use and has been devoid of track for many years.

Gloucester Class 100 Driving Motor Brake Second (DMBS) M51117 was bringing up the rear of a lengthy rake of empty DMU cars stood in platform 5 at Crewe on 9 June 1979. There had been forty two-car Class 100 Power Trailer sets built in two batches by the Gloucester Railway Carriage & Wagon Company between 1956 and 1958.

Plenty of activity on platform 6 at Crewe as two-car Class 175/0 No. 175005, still carrying the old Arriva Trains Wales livery, was garnering custom with the 12.31 Manchester Piccadilly to Milford Haven Transport for Wales (TfW) service on 8 June 2019. The TfW Alstom-built Class 175 Coradia fleet of two- and three-car sets were withdrawn from service during 2023.

One of the exhibits at the Crewe Works Open Day on 22 September 1979, Test Coach 'Iris' (RDB975010) was in the red/blue livery of the Railway Technical Centre at Derby. Built in 1956 as one of a pair of single units (Nos 79900 and 79901), and eventually deemed as nonstandard, No. 79900 was withdrawn from passenger service in 1967 and passed into departmental use. It entered into preservation in 1999 and has since been restored to original 1950s condition as M79900.

TfW three-car Class 175/1 No. 175110 was easing past Beeston Brook with a Llandudno Junction to Crewe ECS on 1 March 2023. The TfW 175 fleet consisted of eleven two-car (Nos 175001–175011) and sixteen three-car sets (Nos 175101–175116). The fleet was replaced by new Class 197 DMUs during 2023, and the entire class of 175s was transferred to GWR in 2025.

TfW Class 197/1 No. 197105 was stood in platform 4 at Chester with the 12.43 Llandudno to Manchester Piccadilly service (1H88) on 7 October 2023. TfW has a fleet of twenty-six of these CAF-built three-car DMUs (Nos 197101–197126).

Three Swindon-built Class 120 CrossCountry DMU sets were stabled at Chester Depot on 9 August 1981. The original fleet of these well-appointed units totalled 194 individual cars, built in several batches between 1957 and 1961 and formed into three-car sets. The last of the well-worn Class 120s were withdrawn in 1989.

With the road set, the driver of Avanti West Coast Class 221 Voyager No. 221113 was getting some fresh air whilst awaiting departure time from Chester with the 263-mile, 10.02 London Euston to Holyhead service (1D84) on 7 October 2023. The AWC fleet of Class 221s were replaced by Class 805 bi-mode units on London Euston to North Wales services during 2024.

TfW Class 150/2 No. 150264 was departing from Hawarden Bridge station and about to cross the River Dee on the impressive Hawarden Bridge whilst working the 09.32 Bidston to Wrexham General service (2J55) on 2 November 2022. The station here is adjacent to the once extensive Shotton steelworks complex. Hawarden Bridge was completed in 1889 for the Manchester, Sheffield & Lincolnshire Railway. The central section of the bridge was once the largest opening span of any swing bridge in the UK at 278 feet.

Running on bullhead rail with wooden sleepers and cast-iron chairs, TfW Class 150/2 No. 150283 was passing signal ML581 as it departed from Bidston with the 14.32 Bidston to Wrexham Central service (2J65) on 19 March 2022. These hourly 'Borderlands Line' diesel services use platform 1 at Bidston station and have a quick turnaround in-between the West Kirby fifteen-minute interval Merseyrail Wirral Line electrics. No. 150283 was amongst the last batch of 150/2 Sprinters built at BREL York in 1987 that went new north of the border to Haymarket Depot at Edinburgh (Nos 150283–150285).

Northern Class 142s Nos 142055 and 142052 were stabled between duties at Liverpool Lime Street on 11 October 2014. The two units were part of a batch of seventeen 142s (Nos 142041–142049 and Nos 142051–142058) adopted by Merseytravel in 1992 and fitted with revised interiors, dot matrix destination displays and finished in Merseyrail yellow livery.

Northern Class 150/1 No. 150141 was stood at Edge Hill with the 12.31 Wigan North Western to Liverpool Lime Street service on 4 October 2014. The station buildings form part of the oldest operational railway station in the world and were extensively restored in 1979 prior to the 150th anniversary of the opening of the Liverpool to Manchester Railway the following year in 1980.

Having run from Manchester Oxford Road via the former Cheshire Lines route, East Midlands Railway (EMR), Regional branded Class 158s Nos 158889 and 158812 were approaching Allerton Junction and Liverpool South Parkway with the 10.57 Norwich to Liverpool Lime Street service on 3 September 2019. The pair of 158s were still in the livery of East Midlands Trains.

With a grimy-looking front end, East Midlands Railway Class 156 No. 156408 was leading the four-car 10.56 Grantham to Liverpool Lime Street service (1R66), heading towards journey's end, passing through Hunts Cross on 5 June 2021. The 156 was one of several EMR 156s transferred to Northern in 2022/23.

Following the end of the three-day 'Rocket 150' cavalcade event at Rainhill on the evening of 26 May 1980, the Army Cadets had been clearing rubbish from the grandstands that had been erected along the line. One highlight that was ignored was the spectacle of the frequent DMU shuttle services to and from Manchester Victoria that ran before and after the cavalcade. The shuttles utilised various DMUs including some borrowed from other parts of the BR network. In this view, a six-car BRCW DMU formation made up of two of Buxton-allocated three-car 104s, with Driving Motor Brake Second (DMBS) M50423 leading, was approaching Rainhill having run ECS from Manchester.

With its first-class saloon downgraded to second, a Derby Class 108 Driving Trailer Second Lavatory (DTSL) and Motor Brake Second (DMBS) No. 53606 were stabled between duties in the carriage sidings at Southport on 29 August 1988.

In Greater Manchester PTE orange livery, Class 142 No. 142002 had just passed through the Steamport Museum boundary gates whilst operating a Steamport to Southport station shuttle service on 29 June 1986 as part of a joint BR/Steamport open day. The first fourteen Class 142s (Nos 142001–142014) were finished in GM orange, which at the time matched the Greater Manchester bus fleet. No. 142002 would eventually become part of the Arriva Trains Wales fleet based at Cardiff Canton Depot.

The rare sight of a Gloucester RC&W Class 122 single unit, M55006, coupled to the rear of a two-car Class 108 DMU departing from Croston with an Ormskirk to Preston service on 5 August 1985. At the time, Newton Heath Depot had a pair of Class 122s allocated for use on the Stockport to Stalybridge services. The former Jubilee Mill complex that forms a backdrop here has now been demolished and replaced with houses.

Substituting for an errant Class 142, a Class 108 two-car DMU had returned to its old stamping ground on 16 May 1992. Formed of cars Nos 54238 and 53956 (LO296), the 08.21 Ormskirk to Preston service had just returned the single-line token at Midge Hall signal box. The unit is about to pass through the derelict platforms of the former station, closed in 1961. A long-time haunt of Class 108s, this was the final visit along this former main line of a first generation DMU.

In a scene that is now history, Avanti West Coast Voyagers Nos 221101 and 221111 were passing Winwick, just north of Warrington, with the 13.16 London Euston to Glasgow Central service (9S77) on 22 August 2023. The leading set, No. 221101, still carries the base white livery from its days with Virgin Trains when it was the only Voyager to be adorned with the later-style white finish, whilst the trailing set, No. 221111, has retained the normal silver base colour.

East Midlands Trains Meridian Class 222 No. 222001 was departing from Warrington Central with the 08.45 Nottingham to Liverpool Lime Street service on 9 April 2011. The 222 was running in place of the usual EMT Class 158s due to increased patronage for the Grand National race meeting being held at Aintree.

With faded BR maroon totems on the gas lamps, a two-car Derby Class 108 DMU formed of cars M52040 and M50933 was stabled between duties in the bay at Wigan Wallgate on 14 August 1977. There was a tail lamp 'stop' marker on the platform and the westbound platform was furnished with 1960s white enamel DMU 'Car stop' signs.

An almost new two-car No. 195022 was approaching platform 1 at Wigan North Western with the 10.32 Preston to Wigan crew training run on 3 March 2020. Northern has a fleet of twenty-five CAF-built Civity Class 195/0 two-car DMUs (Nos 195001–195025).

Following withdrawal from passenger use, redundant Park Royal Class 103 Driving Trailer Composite Lavatory (DTCL) M56156 was converted to a Sandite coach and renumbered in the departmental series as ADB977047. The non-powered car was stabled at Wigan Springs Branch Depot on 12 August 1984.

The tail end of Northern Class 150/1 No. 150109 was passing over Deansgate Lane whilst working the 07.56 Chester to Manchester Piccadilly service (2H34) on 17 February 2024. Located just east of Altrincham, Deansgate Junction is where the Manchester Metrolink runs alongside the national network on the former tracks of the Manchester South Junction & Altrincham Railway (MSJ&A).

Cross Country Class 220 Voyager No. 220021 was passing through Macclesfield with the 06.54 Cardiff Central to Manchester Piccadilly service (1M35) on 12 November 2016.

BR Regional Railways-liveried Metro Cammell Class 101s Nos 101679 and 101681 were arriving at Buxton at the completion of their 25-mile journey with the 17.23 departure from Manchester Piccadilly on 30 May 1996.

Northern Class 150/1s Nos 150144 and 150104 were departing from Furness Vale with the 16.46 Buxton to Manchester Piccadilly service (2B45) on 26 September 2023. The rear of No. 150144 is passing the stone-built station house dating from 1857. On the right is Furness Vale signal box, an LNWR type 4 design that dates from 1887.

Northern Class 142s Nos 142033 and 142042 were stood in the small terminus at Rose Hill Marple, with the 12.14 to Manchester Piccadilly on 19 April 2019. Located on a short 2-mile spur from Marple Wharf Junction, the line to Rose Hill was once part of a through route to Macclesfield that was closed west of here in 1970.

With the Peak Forest Canal in the foreground, Northern Class 195/0 No. 195012 was crossing Marple Viaduct with the 12.14 Sheffield to Manchester Piccadilly service (2S81) on 10 August 2022.

Still carrying Strathclyde PTE livery and branding, First North Western two-car Class 101 No. 101691 formed of cars Nos 53171 and 51253 was departing from Romiley with the 14.25 Manchester Piccadilly to Marple service on 29 September 2001. The routes from Piccadilly to New Mills Central, Marple and Rose Hill Marple became the last regular stamping ground for the Longsight-allocated Class 101 fleet until they were withdrawn in 2003.

Former Transport for Wales and Greater Anglia Class 170/2s, Nos 170207 and 170205, were passing Chinley whilst working the 09.51 Liverpool Lime Street to Norwich East Midlands Trains service (1L09) on 19 September 2024. The lead unit, No. 170207, was in base white livery following transfer from TfW.

An almost new and unbranded Transpennine Express 'Nova 1' bi-mode Class 802/2, No. 802219, was stood at Stalybridge with the 06.03 Newcastle to Liverpool Lime Street service (9M04) on 14 December 2019. TPE have nineteen of these Hitachi-built five-car 'Nova 1' units (Nos 802201–802219). Electrification of the route over the Pennines via Huddersfield will eventually see these trains operating in electric mode only for the entire journey.

The penultimate Siemens-built Class 185, No. 185150 was rolling to a halt at Mossley whilst working the 12.44 Hull to Manchester Piccadilly TransPennine Express service (1K20) on 10 June 2018. The cross-Pennine railway here was constructed by the Huddersfield & Manchester Railway Company and opened in July 1849, by which time the company had become part of the LNWR.

TransPennine Express Class 185s were meeting high in the Pennines at Diggle on 5 February 2019. In the foreground, No. 185114 had just emerged into daylight after passing through the 3-mile 60-yard Standedge Tunnel, with the 08.15 Newcastle to Manchester Airport service (1P18), whilst coming in the opposite direction, No. 185142 was working the 09.25 Liverpool Lime Street to Newcastle service (9E09).

A West Yorkshire PTE refurbished Metro Cammell Class 101 DMU, with Driving Trailer Composite Lavatory (DTCL) car E56220 leading, was running ECS from Marsden on the east side of the 3-mile 60-yard Standedge Tunnel, and was approaching the signal box at Diggle in readiness to cross over to the Up line to return ECS to Marsden from where it would form a service to Huddersfield on 11 August 1979. This was common practice at the time; track rationalisation at Marsden station had removed any crossovers for terminating DMU services, and subsequently they had to travel to Diggle to cross over for the return journey. A third bi-directional platform has since been added at Marsden.

Transport for Wales (TfW) Class 197/1 No. 197105 was running above the new interchange/ bus station as it was passing over Stockport Viaduct with the 09.30 Manchester Piccadilly to Carmarthen service (1V38) on 3 August 2024. TfW has twenty-six CAF-built Civity three-car DMUs (Nos 197101–197126).

Northern Class 142 No. 142030 was entering bay platform 3A at Stockport at the conclusion of its 8-mile run with the 08.46 Stalybridge to Stockport once weekly 'Parliamentary' service (2J44) on 27 July 2019. The service and the corresponding return working, the 09.46 from Stockport to Stalybridge (2J45), were at the time the only two service trains to call at the intermediate stations of Reddish South and Denton. Visible on the right is Stockport No. 2 signal box, dating from 1870. The former LNWR structure (along with Stockport No. 1) controls the busy track layout at Stockport.

Dating from 1960, one of the stylish Swindon-built Class 124 TransPennine DMU sets, with Driving Motor Composite (DMC) E51960 nearest the camera, was stabled at Longsight Depot on 31 August 1980. The 124s were originally five-car units including a buffet car, for use between Liverpool and Hull, but they were reduced to four cars towards the end of their careers, some becoming hybrid units with a mix of Class 124 and Class 123 cars.

A Class 128 Motor Parcels Van, M55990, was stood in platform 6 at Manchester Piccadilly on 18 March 1979. There were ten of these machines built by the Gloucester Railway Carriage & Wagon Company in 1959. They were fitted with a pair of Albion 230-hp engines, and were able to haul additional vans, or work with other blue square coupling DMU sets. The last 128s were withdrawn in 1991.

Seeing out its last days working from Longsight Depot as set LO253, and working on local services from Manchester Piccadilly, a Derby Class 108 formed of cars M54275 and M51421 was awaiting departure from platform 1 at Piccadilly with a service to New Mills Central on 28 February 1992. The final 108s would be withdrawn in 1993. They (and other life-expired first generation units) were kept in service due to the then ongoing problems with the Class 142 fleet.

CrossCountry four-car Class 220 Voyager No. 220030 was departing from Manchester Piccadilly with the 13.27 departure to Reading (1O20) on 14 December 2019.

With the Sackville Street building of Manchester University as a backdrop, TfW Class 175 No. 175003 was about to cross the A6 London Road as it approached platform 13 at Manchester Piccadilly with the 07.45 Llandudno to Manchester Airport service (1D34) on 21 September 2019. The fleet of TfW Class 175 DMUs were withdrawn from service in 2023 and have since been transferred to GWR for use in Devon and Cornwall.

Northern three-car CAF-built Civity Class 195/1 No. 195115 was departing from Manchester Oxford Road with the 12.50 Manchester Airport to Liverpool Lime Street service on 3 August 2019. The almost new unit would travel over the former Cheshire Lines (CLC) route via Warrington Central.

Class 142 No. 142052 had just departed from Manchester Oxford Road on the last leg of its journey with the 16.46 Wigan North Western to Manchester Piccadilly service on 23 July 2019. No. 142052 was one of the seventeen ex-Merseyrail 142s that had been modified/refurbished in 1992. The unit was in service with Northern until early December 2019 and was subsequently scrapped at EMR Kingsbury.

Old and new at a wet Manchester Victoria on 17 October 1991. The two-car Derby Class 108 formed of cars 54247 and 53964 had been given a retro BR green livery in 1986 whilst based at Carlisle, and was initially used on the Settle–Carlisle line. The unit was eventually transferred to Chester Depot, then became Longsight set LO298. Alongside was Class 142 No. 142030 on a service to Wigan Wallgate.

One of the distinctive Newton Heath-allocated Cravens Class 105 power twin formed of cars M50804 and M50765 was stood at Manchester Victoria after arrival from Blackburn on 27 March 1979.

Northern Alstom-built Class 180 Adelante No. 180108 was departing from Bolton with the 14.23 Preston to Hazel Grove service on 22 April 2011. Northern had three Class 180s capable of 125 mph (Nos 180103/106/108) in the fleet between 2008 and 2011. No. 180108 is now part of the Grand Central fleet of Class 180s.

A two-car BRCW Class 104 DMU formed of cars M53499 and M53470 was leading a pair of Class 108s on a six-car Blackpool North to Manchester Victoria service, departing from the market town of Chorley on 30 August 1986. 104s were a common sight on the Blackpool–Manchester route for many years.

A Swindon CrossCountry Class 120 Driving Motor Brake Second (DMBS), M53735, was bringing up the rear of a six-car Manchester Victoria to Blackpool North service stood on the Down slow at Leyland station on 28 December 1985. Running as part of a three-car set, the centre trailer car was a Class 101 Metro Cammell M59528, whilst the other leading Class 120 car was M53680. The unit was eventually withdrawn from Newton Heath depot in May 1986 and subsequently scrapped. The DMU is stood alongside the original low-height North Union Railway stone platform dating from 1838. This is believed to be the oldest platform in the same position along the entire WCML that is still in use.

In Merseyrail livery with First North Western branding, Class 142 No. 142055 was stood at Leyland with the 08.02 Liverpool Lime Street to Blackpool North service on 11 July 1999.

Class 142 No. 142026 was climbing Farington Curve with a Blackpool South to Colne service on 8 September 1990. No. 142026 was one of the thirteen Skippers (Nos 142015–142027) that went new to Plymouth Laira depot in 1985. Their stay in the West Country was brief; by 1988 the fleet was banished north and shared between Newton Heath and Heaton depots. No. 142026 was in service with Northern until late 2019 and was scrapped at Sims Metals at Newport in January 2020.

In unbranded East Midlands livery, Class 156 No. 156415 was stood in platform 2 at Preston awaiting departure with the 19.57 Preston to Colne service on 2 March 2022. The unit was one of several ex-EMR 156s transferred to Northern in 2022.

Still in BR blue/grey livery, Class 101 Sandite two-car DMU No. 960995 was stood in bay platform 4C at Preston station on 28 May 1994. The cars had been renumbered to 997903 (ex-53208) and 997904 (ex-53291). The set had previously been operating from Longsight Depot, numbered LO995. It was converted for Sandite use in 1993, and was withdrawn in 2001 and scrapped in 2003.

An ex-Eastern Region Cravens power trailer Class 105 DMU was awaiting departure in bay platform 3C at Preston with a service to Ormskirk (despite the destination display) on 22 October 1977.

DMUs new and old were stood in Croft Street Sidings adjacent to Preston Power Box on 28 August 1988. From left to right, a shiny new Metro Cammell-built Class 156 Sprinter, No. 156430, with a rare blue/grey-liveried BRCW Class 104 Driving Car, M53534, stood alongside, and on the right, a Pressed Steel-built Class 117, with Driving Motor Brake Second (DMBS) M51372 nearest the camera.

A pair of three-car BRCW Class 104s, with Driving Motor Brake Second M50475 at the rear, were stood at Salwick with the 16.45 Blackpool North to Manchester Victoria service on 28 June 1980. The small single-island platform station located in semi-rural surroundings between Preston and Kirkham still retained its ex-Lancashire & Yorkshire Railway canopy. This once busy section of railway had, until 1966, four tracks along here to cope with the excursion/holiday traffic to and from Blackpool.

With its NHS branding that was applied in 2020, Northern Class 195/1 No. 195111 was passing Kirkham & Wesham running ECS with the 12.19 Blackpool North to Leeds (5B28) on 8 April 2023. The route between Preston and Blackpool North was electrified in 2018.

Class 150/2 No. 150231 was running alongside some departmental wagons in what was once the goods yard at Kirkham & Wesham, as it headed for the Fylde Coast with a Manchester Victoria to Blackpool North service on 3 September 1988. No. 150231 had been one of a large batch of 'odd' numbered BREL York-built 150/2 Sprinters that had gone new to Newton Heath depot the previous year. No. 150231 would eventually be part of the Transport for Wales (TfW) fleet.

With the former Parkinson's biscuit factory dominating the skyline, a Swindon Class 120 hybrid set coupled to a two-car BRCW Class 104 was approaching Kirkham North Junction with Driving Motor Second Lavatory (DMSL) M53694 leading a Manchester Victoria to Blackpool North service on 30 June 1984. The centre car was a Class 101 Metro Cammell Trailer Second Lavatory (59054).

In its original but well-worn BR Provincial Services livery, Class 150/1 No. 150137 was stood in the Blackpool suburbs at Layton with the 15.20 Stockport to Blackpool North service on 6 June 1992. The 150 had been new from BREL York in 1985 and its first home was at Derby Etches Park. By 1992, No. 150137 was allocated to Newton Heath Depot, where it is still part of the Northern fleet.

In the revised Greater Manchester livery and with its 'Regional Railways' branding partly blanked out, First North Western Class 150/1 No. 150137 was arriving at Blackpool North with the 08.56 departure from Buxton on 24 October 1997.

In its original Express livery, Class 158 No. 158776 was departing from Blackpool North with the 10.47 service to York on 24 October 1997. No. 158776 is now part of a three-car Great Western Railway (GWR) Class 158/0 No. 158958.

First TransPennine Express Class 185 No. 185130, in its First Group Dymamic Lines livery, was amongst the semaphores whilst departing from Blackpool North with the 10.44 to Manchester Airport on 16 May 2015. The terminus at Blackpool North has since had the platforms completely rebuilt, and 185s no longer visit the Fylde coast.

A worn-looking Class 104 DMU formed of cars M53451 and M53518 was stood at Squires Gate with a Blackpool South to Colne service on 15 October 1988. The Coast Line from Blackpool South to Kirkham had fallen on hard times, with just a single track remaining on this once busy route that in the days gone by buzzed with activity. Despite being close to the then Pontins holiday camp and Blackpool Airport (both now history) the facilities at Squires Gate had been reduced to a bare platform. The 104 was in its last period of extended operation due to ongoing problems with the Class 142 fleet.

The Fisons Weedkilling Train had been stabled in the yard of what was once Lostock Hall MPD on the evening of 18 May 1978. The spray coach, numbered FA99900, had been converted from a Gloucester Railway Carriage & Wagon Company Class 100 Driving Trailer Composite Lavatory (DTCL) DMU car E56315 that had been built in 1958.

Three-car Class 150/0 No. 150001, in de-branded GWR green livery, was passing Lostock Hall Junction with the 10.20 Newton Heath TMD to Blackburn King Street ECS working (5T69) on 21 July 2020. No. 150001 was one of a pair of prototype three-car Class 150s built at BREL York in 1984. For evaluation purposes at the time, No. 150001 was fitted with Cummins engines and Voith hydraulic transmission, whilst No. 150002 was equipped with Perkins (Rolls-Royce) engines and SCG automatic gearboxes. Due to the unreliability of the equipment on No. 150002, it was eventually fitted with engines and final drive as per No. 150001. Both units were transferred from GWR to Northern at Newton Heath Depot in the early part of 2020.

Following an overnight heavy snowfall, a Newton Heath-allocated Class 105 power twin formed of cars M50761 and M50788 was stood at Bamber Bridge with a Colne to Preston service on 27 January 1979. These Cravens units were a familiar sight on the former L&YR routes in the North West in the 1970s.

Contrasting liveries at Blackburn on 28 September 2018, as ex-Greater Anglia Class 153 No. 153305 in base white livery and Class 150/1 No. 150120 in de-branded First Great Western livery were commencing their 34-mile journey with the 10.18 Blackburn to Rochdale service (via Darwen & Manchester Victoria).

On 23 June 1979, the summer Saturday-only Blackpool North to Castleford service was formed of ten cars. The leading car was Calder Valley Class 110 Driving Motor Composite E51833. The Class 110 fleet of thirty three-car sets, built by BRCW and introduced in 1961, were fitted with Rolls-Royce 180-hp engines to cope with the gradients of the former L&Y Calder Valley route between Manchester/Bradford/Leeds. They had the highest power to weight ratio of all the BR first generation DMU fleet. The units were familiar visitors to Blackpool; in the 1970s there was a daily Bradford–Blackpool North service always formed of a single three-car set, and at the time was the only regular timetabled passenger train to run over the Copy Pit route.

Former Bedford–St Pancras Diesel Hydraulic Red Triangle DMU driving cars Nos 55972 (51611) and 55982 (51596), running as parcel unit 912, were passing Daisyfield level crossing at Blackburn with a diverted Workington to Manchester mail service on 29 March 1986. The unit had a CCT van as a tail load. There were twenty-two former Bed-Pan Hydraulic driving cars that were converted and formed into eleven two-car parcel/mail/newspaper units and given set numbers 910–920.

With the ground signal cleared, Northern Class 158 No. 158903 and Class 153 No. 153378 were stood on the Down line at Horrocksford Junction, running ECS as the 10.58 Clitheroe to Clitheroe reversing move (5J21) on 5 May 2021. The pair of units had arrived at nearby Clitheroe station with the 09.17 departure from Rochdale (2N54) and after reversing and accessing the Up line at Horrocksford Junction, would form the 11.25 Clitheroe to Rochdale service (2J21). To the left, the signal (HJ4) controls the exit from the cement works branch.

The tail end of Northern Class 158 No. 158853 was passing over Atlas Street as it arrived at Darwen with the 10.41 Manchester Victoria to Clitheroe service (2N55) on 7 February 2020. Class 158s no longer work services in East Lancashire.

With the terraced houses on Chapel Street as a backdrop, Northern Class 156 No. 156421 was passing over Barkerhouse Road/Chaffers Siding level crossing as it exited Nelson with the last leg of the 12.54 Preston to Colne service on 21 May 2019.

Northern Class 195/1 No. 195105 was hurrying southbound along the WCML at Woodacre, between Scorton and Garstang & Catterall, with the 16.00 Windermere to Manchester Airport service (1C58) on 19 April 2023. Visible in the background is the M6 motorway between junctions 32 and 33, which parallels the railway for many miles.

Virgin Trains Class 221 Voyager No. 221110 was departing from platform 4 at Lancaster with the 12.43 London Euston to Edinburgh service (9S70) on 20 August 2019 – a long journey for a diesel-powered train running 'under the wires' for the entirety of its route.

Northern Class 142 No. 142036 was crossing the River Lune as it was departing from Lancaster with the 15.27 service to Morecambe on 6 April 2019. No. 142036 survives in preservation – a long way from its former operating territory at the East Kent Railway.

In its 'RAF 100' livery, Heaton-allocated Class 156 No. 156480 was departing from platform 1 at Bare Lane with the 4-mile 14.51 Lancaster to Morecambe service (2C71) on 29 January 2022. The two lines here are both single bi-directional individually signalled tracks, installed to increase capacity at the small terminus at nearby Morecambe.

With the shadows lengthening on a fine spring evening, TransPennine Express Class 185 No. 185105 was running at speed at Hest Bank on the shore of Morecambe Bay whilst working the 19.10 Manchester Airport to Oxenholme service on 26 May 2019. TPE has fifty-one of these Siemens-built DMUs that were built in 2005/2006 (Nos 185101–185151).

In its original West Yorkshire PTE livery, three-car Class 144 No. 144022 was awaiting departure from Carnforth with the 74-mile 14.17 Leeds to Morecambe service on 10 August 1999. No. 144022 was in service with Northern until 2020, when it passed into preservation, and is currently located north of the border on the Keith & Dufftown Railway.

In de-branded First Group livery, Doyen Class 175/1 No. 175101 was arriving at Carnforth with the 14.51 Barrow-in-Furness to Manchester Airport service on 30 May 2004. The Class 175 fleet had been transferred from First North Western to the Wales & Borders franchise in October 2003, but eleven units were sub-leased back to FNW, although the service(s) seen here had been transferred to First TransPennine Express in February 2004. Class 175s were eventually replaced by new TPE Class 185s in 2006.

Northern Class 156 No. 156469 was arriving at Arnside whilst working the 92-mile 15.49 Maryport to Lancaster service on 26 May 2019. The 156 was a long way from its home depot at Heaton on Tyneside.

A pair of Derby Class 108 DMUs, with Driving Trailer Second Lavatory (DTSL) M56264 leading, were approaching Grange-over-Sands with a Barrow-in-Furness to Preston service on 12 April 1982. 108s were synonymous with the Cumbrian Coast route in the 1970/80s, the sets having bars over the door droplights due to restricted clearances on the section between Maryport and Carlisle.

In unbranded green stripe Regional Railways North West livery, First North Western Class 156 No. 156424 was awaiting departure from Grange-over-Sands with the 13.00 Barrow-in-Furness to Lancaster (via Morecambe) service on 3 May 1998.

Running alongside the scenic Cumbrian coast, Northern Class 156 No. 156421 had just passed through the small station at Nethertown whilst working the 120-mile 11.07 Carlisle to Lancaster service (2C50) on 27 December 2018.

Restored to their original BR green livery on the heritage Lakeside & Haverthwaite Railway, BRCW Class 110 driving cars E52077 and E52071 were stood at the Lake District terminus at Lakeside with the 17.48 service to Haverthwaite on 24 May 1997.

With its NHS branding that was applied in 2020, Northern Class 158 No. 158860 was stood at Bentham with the 14.32 Morecambe to Leeds service (2Y01) on 2 May 2022. The station building dates from 1954 and is in use as an information centre, toilets and a community hub. The background is dominated by the art deco-style office block of the Angus Firefighting equipment company on Station Road.

In the short-lived 'refurbished' white with blue stripe livery, a Leeds Neville Hill Depot-allocated two-car Metro Cammell Class 101 DMU was approaching Settle Junction with a Leeds to Morecambe service on 13 May 1978.

Northern three-car Class 158 No. 158755 was approaching Settle Junction with the 13.40 Carlisle to Leeds service (1E65) on 7 September 2022. The pair of tracks on the left are the 'Little North Western' route to Carnforth via Wennington and are used by Leeds–Morecambe–Leeds services. Northern has a fleet of eight three-car 158s (Nos 158752–158759).

Northern two-car Class 144 No. 144002 was about to depart from Long Preston whilst working the 13.17 Bentham to Leeds service on 1 April 2018. The small station serves the village located on the nearby A65 trunk road. Following withdrawal in 2020, No. 144002 has since been repurposed as a library and classroom at a school in Northallerton.

At the rear of the 'Long Thin Drag' railtour on 12 April 1986, a pair of Southern Region Class 201 Hastings power cars were placed at the rear of the main train as insurance should problems arise during the lengthy journey from the south coast to Carlisle. Sets 1032 and 1011 formed the main section of the train, with power cars from set 1001 bringing up the rear as the tour passed Hellifield. The tour was organised by Hertfordshire Railtours & The Southern Electric Group, departing from Hastings at 04.50, to London Victoria, where departure was at 06.52. The units came back from Carlisle over the WCML via Shap.

Still carrying Scotrail Saltire vinyls, Class 158 No. 158786 had just passed over the B6255 Ingleton to Hawes road as it departed from Ribblehead with the 15.18 Leeds to Carlisle service on 19 June 2019. The unit was one of several 158s transferred south of the border to Northern in 2018/19.

High in the Yorkshire Dales at England's highest main line station, there was still frost on the sleepers just before midday on 8 December 1987 as a two-car Derby Class 108 DMU formed of cars 54249 and 53966 was departing from Dent with the 10.05 Carlisle to Leeds stopping service.

Passing a leaning signal, Northern three-car Class 158 No. 158756 was getting underway from the former junction station at Garsdale on its 112.79-mile journey with the 09.20 Leeds to Carlisle service (1M53) on 26 April 2023.

In its original BR Provincial Services livery, Heaton-allocated Class 143 No. 143605 (55646 and 55671) was stood at Oxenholme with a service to Windermere on 8 March 1992. This was a brief period when the 10-mile Windermere branch was operated by Class 143s. There had been twenty-five 143s constructed by Hunslet-Barclay using Alexander bus bodies in 1985, for use in the North East. In later years, No. 143605 eventually passed to Arriva Trains Wales, but has since been scrapped.

The view along Sharps Lane as the tail end of Class 185 No. 185124 was clearing Burneside Lower Crossing whilst working the 08.25 Manchester Airport to Windermere First TransPennine Express service on 23 May 2015. All trains observe a 5-mph speed limit whilst traversing this narrow lane. TPE ceased working the Windermere branch services in 2016 and the scenic line is now part of the Northern network.

At a run-down-looking Windermere terminus on a wet summer's day, Cravens Class 105 power trailers M50385 and M56118 were the rear two cars of the four-car Oxenholme to Windermere branch service on 29 June 1980. Since 1986, this part of the station has become part of a supermarket.

High in the Cumbrian Fells, First TransPennine Express Class 185 No. 185128 was passing Greenholme whilst climbing towards Shap Summit with the 16.00 Manchester Airport to Edinburgh service on 29 September 2013. By the end of 2013, new Siemens-built Class 350/4 EMUs had been introduced on these services and another chapter in the varied history of West Coast Main Line motive power had started.

With the windscreen washers in operation, Virgin Class 221Voyager No. 221113 was stood at Penrith with the 10.00 Glasgow Central to London Euston service (9M53) on 14 May 2019.

Former Scotrail Class 156 No. 156496 was departing from Carlisle with the 19.09 Northern service to Barrow-in-Furness (2C50) on 7 September 2019. The 85-mile journey along the Cumbrian coast would take just over 2.25 hours to complete. The 156 was still wearing the then obsolete Barbie First Group livery.

A Scottish Region Derby Class 107 DMU formed of cars SC52028, SC59799 and SC52002 had arrived in bay platform 7 at Carlisle with a service from Kilmarnock on 25 March 1979. There had been twenty-six Class 107 sets built at Derby in 1960, the fleet spending their entire working lives on Scottish Region services.

With Scotrail Class 156 No. 156507 stabled in platform 8, LNER Class 800/1 bi-mode Azuma No. 800110 was stood in platform 3 at Carlisle with the diverted 06.28 Edinburgh to London Kings Cross service on 28 September 2019. Having worked from Edinburgh to Carlisle using electric power, the 800 would work forwards to Newcastle on the non-electrified Tyne Valley route using diesel power.

Class 142 No. 142021 was departing from Brampton with the 108-mile 15.28 Carlisle to Middlesbrough service on 8 October 2016. The distant signal was controlled from nearby Milton signal box.

Scotrail Class 156 No. 156501 was approaching Haydon Bridge whilst working the 07.07 Glasgow Central to Newcastle service (1E95) on 8 October 2016.

Overlooked by the Castle Keep, CrossCountry Class 220 Voyager No. 220028 was departing from the city of Newcastle with the 06.30 Penzance to Morpeth service (1S45) on 28 September 2019. With an on-time arrival at Morpeth at 16.48, the Voyager completed a 10-hour 18-minute marathon.

In the old First Group Barbie livery, former Scotrail Class 156 No. 156447 had just passed over the busy A167 as it exited Newcastle with the Northern 12.41 Newcastle to Whitby service (2N28) on 7 September 2019.

Heaton-allocated Class 142 No. 142071 was about to cross the River Tyne on the High Level Bridge as it departed from Newcastle Central with the well-filled 10.56 Hexham to Danby service (2N20) on 7 September 2019. Designed by Robert Stephenson, the High Level Bridge was opened by Queen Victoria on 15 August 1849. No. 142071 was subsequently scrapped in 2021.

Northern Class 158 No. 158843 was threading its way out of Newcastle with the 08.29 Loughborough to Heaton Depot ECS move on 7 September 2019. The 158 had been receiving attention at the former Brush Works and was returning back to its home depot.

Former Scotrail Class 156 No. 156447 was approaching Pelaw Junction with the 14.56 Hexham to Battersby service (2N34) on 28 September 2019.

Having just passed through St Peters, Northern Class 158 No. 158793 was crossing over the River Wear on the Monkwearmouth Bridge as it was approaching Sunderland with the 09.40 Newcastle to Hunthorpe service on 22 September 2022. The tracks here are part of the national network, but are shared with the Tyne & Wear Metro. The signs on the right are a reminder that the Metro system was the first railway network in the UK to adopt metric units of measurement.

Northern Class 156 No. 156472 was approaching Hartlepool with the 47.36-mile 08.16 Middlesbrough to Newcastle service (1J00) on 20 June 2024. The area immediately behind the 156 was once the site of Hartlepool MPD. No. 156472 is one of the large fleet of Northern 156s allocated to Heaton Depot for use across the North East.

TransPennine Express Class 185 No. 185129 was arriving at Darlington with the 161-mile 08.17 Manchester Airport to Newcastle service (1P17) on 10 October 2018. In platform 2, No. 142094 was awaiting departure with the 10.40 service to Saltburn (2D26). No. 142094 has survived into preservation at the Weardale Railway.

Sixty-five feet above the River Tees and the town of Yarm, TransPennine Express Class 185s Nos 185105 and 185129 were passing over the forty-three arches of Yarm viaduct whilst working the 12.51 Saltburn to Manchester Airport service (1P74) on 20 June 2024. The viaduct was completed in 1852 for the Leeds Northern Railway.

Class 142 No. 142088 was awaiting departure from Thornaby with the 12.11 Bishop Auckland to Saltburn service (2D36) on 10 October 2018.

With the famous Transporter Bridge dominating the skyline, TransPennine Express Class 185s Nos 185125 and 185127 were accelerating away from Middlesbrough with the 10.07 Redcar Central to Manchester Airport service (1P68) on 2 February 2022.

With the industrial landscape of Teeside as a backdrop, No. 142093 was approaching Middlesbrough with the 13.18 Darlington to Saltburn service on 10 October 2018. The unit was one of the last 142/1s built in 1987 and was in service with Northern until December 2019. It was scrapped in 2020.

Northern No. 142023 was stood in the basic two-platform terminus at Saltburn-by-the-Sea awaiting departure with the 16.17 service to Darlington on 9 October 2018. One of the former Devon & Cornwall 'Skippers', No. 142023 has survived into preservation at the Plym Valley Railway in Devon.

In First Group Dynamic Lines livery, TransPennine Express Class 185 No. 185126 was running at speed through the small station at Thirsk on the ECML whilst forming the 12.10 Newcastle to Manchester Airport service on 16 February 2014.

Following a period out of use and storage, a Metro Cammell Class 101 two-car DMU formed of cars E50256 and E56343 was stood at Leeming Bar on the Wensleydale Railway on 15 February 2023.

TransPennine Express Class 185 No. 185126 was passing momentarily across Onhams Lane at Kirkham Abbey whilst working the 11.17 York to Scarborough service (1E29) on 12 October 2022. Visible in the background are the ruins of Kirkham Abbey that date from around 1122.

In the then obsolete Northern Spirit livery, First TransPennine Express Class 158s Nos 158769 and 158766 were stabled in the terminus at Scarborough on 27 August 2006. From the following day, new Class 185s replaced 158s on services between Scarborough, York and beyond.

In the East Riding of Yorkshire, former Scotrail Class 170/4 Turbostar No. 170461 was passing over Wansford Road level crossing as it departed from Driffield with the 10.57 Sheffield to Scarborough service (1W43) on 15 October 2021. Northern has a fleet of sixteen 170/4s that were transferred from Scotrail in 2018.

With both units in the obsolete liveries of their former operators, First North Western and Northern Spirit, Class 158 No. 158753 was departing from the East Yorkshire seaside resort of Bridlington with the 14.08 Scarborough to Sheffield (via Hull) service on 27 August 2006. No. 156487 was stabled between duties in bay platform 6. Both units were carrying the small white temporary 'Northern' branding.

With temporary stop blocks on both Up and Down tracks, TransPennine Express Class 185s Nos 185123 and 185149 were stood at Selby on 1 September 2014. The 185s had arrived with the 09.41 Manchester Piccadilly to Selby service, and were stood with the 11.10 return working. The route through Selby was blocked from 27 July until 7 September 2014 whilst the swing bridge across the River Ouse was refurbished. The space where the through lines were once located in the days when Selby was on the ECML is clearly visible.

A Swindon-built InterCity Class 123 Driving Motor Brake Second (DMBS) E52087 was bringing up the rear of a Manchester Piccadilly to Hull service at Selby on 12 September 1981. The former Western Region car had become part of a Class 123/124 hybrid set allocated to Hull Botanic Gardens. The full four-car formation was E52087 (123), E59767 (124), E59765 (124) and E51964 (124). The 123s were the last of the BR first generation DMUs to be built in 1963.

Hull Trains bi-mode Class 802/3 Paragon No. 802304 was awaiting departure from Selby with the 10.50 Beverley to London Kings Cross service (1A92) on 5 September 2021. Hull Trains has five of these AT300 Hitachi-built 802/3s (Nos 802301–802305) that are fitted with diesel engines for use on non-electrified routes.

First TransPennine Express Class 170/3 Turbostar No. 170306 was passing through Gilberdyke with the 09.42 Manchester Piccadilly to Hull on 19 March 2011. Between 2006 and 2016 TPE operated a fleet of nine 170/3s. All are now part of the Chiltern Railways fleet of Class 168/3s, with No. 170306 renumbered to 168326.

Hull Trains Class 180 No. 180113 was approaching Broomfleet with the 15.18 Hull to London Kings Cross service on 30 April 2011. The four Hull Trains five-car Alstom-built Class 180s (Nos 180109/110/111/113) were replaced by Hitachi Class 802/3 bi-mode units in 2020, with the 180s being transferred to East Midlands Railway.

Class 142 No. 142054 was departing from Hull with the well-patronised 12.03 Northern service to York on 21 September 2013. No. 142054 was one of seventeen 142s that had been adopted by Merseyrail in 1992.

In the Vale of York and with the fields in the background still covered in early morning mist, CrossCountry Voyagers Nos 220030 and 221135 were running southbound at Shipton-by-Beningbrough whilst working the 06.24 Newcastle to Reading service (1V83) on 5 September 2023.

In its original West Yorkshire PTE Verona green and buttermilk livery, Class 141 No. 141007 (55508 and 55528) had arrived at York with a service from Leeds via Harrogate on 16 April 1988. The unit would be later refurbished and renumbered to 141108. The 141s featured the narrow body of the Leyland National bus and were not particularly pleasant machines to ride in, and historically they were the first production BR second generation DMUs introduced in 1984.

With its former headcode box panelled over, Metro Cammell Class 111 Driving Motor Composite Lavatory (DTCL) E51552 was stood at York with a service to Scarborough on 15 September 1978. There were ten three-car Class 111s fitted with headcode boxes for the North Eastern Region introduced in 1959/1960. All were fitted with Rolls-Royce 180-hp diesel engines.

In First Group Dynamic Lines livery, First TransPennine Express Class 185 No. 185109 was crossing the River Ouse as it arrived at York with the 08.48 Scarborough to Liverpool Lime Street service on 22 September 2012. 185s have been a familiar sight on the York to Scarborough route since 2006.

Northern three-car Class 158 No. 158759 was stood at Church Fenton with the 18.05 York to Blackpool North service on 26 May 2012. Church Fenton was located on the original East Coast Main Line between 1850 and 1871, when the more direct route was opened via Selby.

Former BR Class 108 cars 54207 and 59142 were stabled in one of the Appleby-Frodingham Railway Preservation Society sidings within the British Steel complex at Scunthorpe on 11 March 2017. The non-powered DMU cars are used as hauled stock for short passenger tours around the steelworks.

Northern two-car Class 144 No. 144013 was departing from Althorpe with the last leg of the 12.24 Sheffield to Scunthorpe service on 19 November 2016. The 144 was about to pass over the impressive King George V bascule bridge that takes both the railway and the A18 over the River Trent. Opened in May 1916, it was last raised in 1956.

Having travelled down the 1,375-foot-long pier from New Holland Pier Head, a Derby Class 114 DMU formed of cars E56043 and E50001, in refurbished livery, was stood at New Holland Town with a service to Cleethorpes on 28 September 1980. These two cars formed the first BR post-Modernisation Plan DMU set when they had been new in 1956. The forty-nine 114 sets were synonymous with services in Lincolnshire for much of their working lives.

Saturday afternoon life was resuming along Howe Lane in the village of Goxhill in North Lincolnshire following the arrival of East Midlands Railway Class 153s Nos 153384 and 153357 with the 14.54 Cleethorpes to Barton-on-Humber service (2F91) on 4 September 2021.

On a warm spring afternoon in rural north-east Lincolnshire, Northern Class 153 No. 153363 was arriving at Thornton Abbey with the 13.58 Barton-on-Humber to Cleethorpes service on 30 April 2011. No. 153363 was in service with Northern until 2021 and has since been scrapped. In 2011, the Barton branch was an isolated part of the Northern network, but since 2021 has been operated by East Midlands Railway.

A line-up of various DMUs at the seaside terminus at Cleethorpes on 30 August 2014. Class 185 No. 185133 was stood with the 15.26 First TransPennine Express service to Manchester Airport; Northern Class 153 No. 153301 was stabled in between working services to and from Barton-on-Humber; and Northern Class 142 No. 142070 was awaiting departure with the Saturday-only 15.20 service to Sheffield.

Northern Class 144 No. 144006 was departing from the market town of Brigg with the Saturdays-only 11.54 Sheffield to Cleethorpes service (2H05) on 7 March 2020. The level crossing gates here were replaced by lifting barriers in March 2020.

A colourful combination at Barnetby on 30 April 2011, with East Midlands Trains Class 153s No. 153379 in Central Trains livery and No. 153355 arriving with a Newark to Grimsby Town service. No. 153379 became part of the Network Rail Class 153 fleet, whilst No. 153355 is stored out of use at Ely Papworth Sidings.

First TransPennine Express Class 170/3 Turbostar No. 170303 was passing South Milford with a Hull to Manchester Piccadilly service on 3 May 2014.

Northern three-car Class 158 No. 158754 was departing from Micklefield with the 14.13 York to Blackpool North service on 12 May 2012. The 158 is passing over what was once the A1 Trunk Road – 'The Great North Road' – that was once traversed by horse-drawn stagecoaches that ran between London and York. Micklefield village was bypassed in 1960. The bridge spanning the road is the original Leeds & Selby Railway structure dating from 1834.

In refurbished white with blue stripe livery, Derby Class 108 Driving Trailer Composite Lavatory (DTCL) E56198 was the lead vehicle of a four-car working to Leeds. Here it is stood at Knottingley station on 5 May 1980.

In Arriva-branded Regional Railways livery, Class 142 No. 142081 was arriving at Poppleton with the 08.29 Leeds to York (via Harrogate) service on 5 July 2001. In 2002, No. 142081 was one of several Arriva 142s transferred to South Wales in exchange for some Class 150/2 Sprinters. No. 142081 was in service with Arriva Trains Wales/TfW until December 2020.

Northern Class 150/2 No. 150226 was arriving at Hammerton with the 15.11 York to Leeds (via Harrogate) service on 12 November 2011. The different colour scheme of each car was due to their previous use as centre cars in different West Midlands-liveried Class 150/1 sets. No. 150226 was reformed as a two-car set when transferred to Northern in 2011.

Having carried its last passengers, a Cravens Class 105 DMU formed of cars 53381 and 54439 had been relegated to mail and parcels duties, seeing out its last few months in traffic before withdrawal stabled between duties at Leeds Neville Hill Depot on 15 March 1987.

Newly delivered from BREL York and without a yellow front end, Class 150/2 No. 150232 was stabled at Leeds Neville Hill Depot on 15 March 1987. The first batches of Class 150/2 Sprinters were split between Neville Hill (even-numbered units) and Newton Heath (odd-numbered units). In later years No. 150232 became part of the GWR fleet.

Still carrying its WYPTE/Pacer headboard from its press launch in December 1986, Class 144 No. 144001 was stabled inside the depot at Leeds Neville Hill on 15 March 1987. No. 144001 was the first of twenty-three 144s that had bodywork built by W. Alexander. Following withdrawal in 2020, the two cars of No. 144001 went their separate ways, 55801 going to Airedale General Hospital and 55824 going to the platform 1 project at Huddersfield station.

With a narrowboat in Office Lock, Northern Class 150/2 No. 150201 was crossing the Leeds & Liverpool Canal as it departed from Leeds with the 11.48 service to Sheffield (2N12) on 14 September 2021.

Stored out of use, Class 140 No. 140001 and Class 141 No. 141001 were stabled at Leeds Holbeck Depot on 15 March 1987. No. 140001 was the prototype Pacer using Leyland National bus bodies. Built in 1981, the two-car set was demonstrated across the UK as a taste of things to come. Withdrawn in 1986, it is now preserved on the Keith & Dufftown Railway. No. 141001 was the first of the second generation DMUs and when new was finished in Barrow Corporation (bus) blue rather than BR Rail blue, as it was the closest match available at the Leyland factory at Workington when built. The twenty 141s were the only production series Pacers to have the narrow bus-style body with 2+2 seating. No. 141001 was eventually renumbered to 141102 following refurbishment, and was exported to Iran in 2001.

Northern Class 158/9 No. 158910 was stood in platform 1 at Bradford Interchange with the 13.03 Huddersfield to Leeds service on 5 March 2019. No. 158901 was one of ten two-car 158/9s (Nos 158901–158910) that had been ordered by the West Yorkshire PTE and delivered in 1992.

Alongside the huge stone retaining wall with Edward Street above, No. 158787 was getting underway from Bradford Interchange with the 13.07 Leeds to Huddersfield service on 5 March 2019.

Grand Central Class 180 Zephyr No. 180107 was awaiting departure from Bradford Interchange with the 208-mile 15.22 service to London Kings Cross on 24 March 2012. Grand Central has a fleet of ten five-car 180s.

Driving car No. 60493 of Grand Central Class 221 Voyager No. 221143 was stood in platform 2 at Bradford Interchange on 30 December 2024. No. 221143 had worked into Bradford with the 10.57 departure from London Kings Cross (1D71) and would return to the capital with the 14.49 departure from Bradford Interchange (1A67). No. 221143 is one of a pair of ex-Virgin Trains Voyagers that are operated by Grand Central alongside their fleet of Class 180s.

Northern Class 144s Nos 144010, 144013, 144011 and 144021 were stored on Keighley & Worth Valley Railway metals at Keighley station on 24 May 2020. Following the Covid-19 lockdown and subsequent fall in passenger numbers, Northern moved eighteen Class 144s to Keighley for temporary safe-keeping/storage on the then dormant heritage line.

With Driving Motor Brake Second (DMBS) 53971 at the rear, a Neville Hill-allocated three-car Class 108 DMU was stood on the Up main alongside Broughton Road Sidings at Skipton during a reversal with a service from Bradford Forster Square on 5 January 1991. The formation, which included three brake vehicles, was a temporary stopgap formation due to a shortage of units.

Complete with its paraffin tail lamp still in position, a refurbished liveried Derby Class 108 two-car DMU formed of cars E50605 and E56199 was stood at Ilkley with a service for Leeds on 9 August 1980. The station still retained its 1950s BR North Eastern Region enamel signage in Tangerine and was also gas-lit. On the extreme right of this view, where the hole in the wall is located, were once the through platforms in the days when Ilkley was on the route to Skipton via Addingham and Bolton Abbey, the western end of which now forms the Embsay & Bolton Abbey Steam Railway. The line beyond Ilkley closed in 1965.

With the 1,105-yard Beacon Hill Tunnel dating from 1849, and the stone cottages on Baldwin Terrace in the background, Northern Class 155 No. 155341 was arriving at Halifax with the 15.07 Leeds to Manchester Victoria service on 24 March 2012. The small fleet of seven ex-WYPTE 155s (155341–155347) were then regular performers on the ex-L&Y Calder Valley route across the Pennines. The stone building behind the leading car of the 155 is part of the former Rowntree-Mackintosh chocolate factory, now part of Nestle UK. The Halifax factory currently produces 'Quality Street' and 'After Eight' chocolates.

First TransPennine Express Class 185 No. 185101 was getting underway from Huddersfield with the 07.15 Liverpool Lime Street to Scarborough service on 29 September 2012.

Northern Class 150/2 No. 150210 was awaiting departure from Huddersfield with the 09.23 service to Bradford Interchange on 29 September 2012. No. 150210 was one of the former West Midlands 150s transferred to Northern in the autumn of 2011.

Northern Class 158s Nos 158793 and 158908 were stood at Ravensthorpe with the 09.53 Wigan North Western to Leeds service (2I09) on 17 August 2022, as TransPennine Express Class 802/2 'Nova 1' No. 802205 was passing with the 09.47 Newcastle to Liverpool Lime Street service (9M20). The 802 was running on diesel power, but the forthcoming electrification of the old LNWR route across the Pennines will enable these units to complete the entire journey 'under the wires'.

With the Huddersfield Narrow Canal basin in the foreground, TransPennine Express Class 185 No. 185132 was approaching the eastern portal of the 3-mile 60-yard Standedge Tunnel whilst working the 11.18 Newcastle to Manchester Airport service (1P24) on 5 February 2019.

Hull Trains Class 180 No. 180110 was hurrying along the ECML on the approach to Joan Croft Junction with 09.06 Hull to London Kings Cross service (1A92) on 12 May 2019.

In Strathclyde PTE orange and black livery, Metro Cammell Class 101 Driving Car 53160 was awaiting attention at Doncaster Works on 12 July 1992. Following overhaul, 53160 was finished in Regional Railways livery and became part of set 101685. In 1994, the car became part of the retro BR green-liveried three-car Class 101 (53160, 59539 and 53164).

Three Class 129 Motor Parcel Vans were built by Cravens of Sheffield in 1958 (M55997-55999). All were withdrawn from service in 1973 but one, M55997, survived as a research vehicle at the Railway Technical Centre at Derby renumbered RDB975385 – Laboratory 9. The car became a test bed for Hydrostatic Drive in 1980, but was withdrawn for a second time in 1984 and was subsequently scrapped. The unique vehicle was awaiting repair at Doncaster Works on 4 February 1979.

The Eastern Region General Managers saloon formed of a Gloucester Class 100 DMU was stood at Doncaster on 13 February 1987. The set was formed of cars 975664 (ex-E51122) and 975637 (ex-E56300), and it was the only first generation DMU to be painted in Provincial Services Sprinter livery as applied to the Class 150/1 fleet when new. Unfortunately, the set was scrapped in 1990.

In its bright yellow livery promoting the Tour de France, Northern Class 158 No. 158849 was arriving at Doncaster with the 09.41 Sheffield to Scarborough (via Bridlington) service on 15 August 2015.

Simultaneous arrivals at Doncaster on 17 August 2021, as East Midlands Railway Class 170/5 Turbostar No. 170532 on the 07.31 Peterborough to Doncaster service (2K06), and TransPennine Express Class 185s Nos 185130 and 185127 with the 08.18 Manchester Piccadilly to Cleethorpes (1B68) were running side by side.

In West Yorkshire PTE Metro Train livery, Class 141 No. 141109 (55529 and 55509) was easing its way into Penistone with the 15.27 Huddersfield to Sheffield service on 27 August 1993. Introduced in 1984, the twenty Class 141s (Nos 141001–141020) were the first production series of second generation DMUs built. They were reworked by Hunslet-Barclay in 1988/89 and renumbered in the 141/1 series. The last would be withdrawn from service in 1997, but No. 141109 was one of twelve 141s exported to Iran in 2001/2002.

Northern Class 150/2 No. 150271 was arriving at Mexborough with the 22.5-mile, 11.05 Sheffield to Adwick service (2R24) on 1 August 2024. Northern has a fleet of twenty-five Class 150/2s.

CrossCountry Class 220 Voyager No. 220022 was awaiting departure from Sheffield with a service to Birmingham New Street on 19 March 2011. The thirty-four four-car 220s were originally ordered by Virgin Trains and entered service in 2000/01. When Virgin lost the CrossCountry franchise in 2007, all of the 220s passed to Arriva CrossCountry and they have been a familiar sight from the south coast to the Midlands, the North and Scotland, no doubt clocking up some impressive mileages over the years.

In a daily scene which is now history, Northern Pacers were passing at Rotherham Central on 15 June 2019. On the left, No. 144008 was arriving with the 14.15 Sheffield to Leeds service, whilst on the right No. 142096 was getting underway with the 12.53 Hull to Sheffield. The overhead wires here are for the Sheffield Supertram services, which run from nearby Parkgate to Sheffield Cathedral and use this short section of Network Rail route with Class 399 'Train Trams'.

With its duties over for the day, Mobile Track Assessment two-car Class 150 Sprinter DB999601 and DB999600 was stabled for the night in Dock Street Sidings at Preston on 9 September 1990. The unit was built at BREL York using the Class 150/1 series bodyshell in 1987 and was a one-off unit. It has since been painted in Network Rail yellow livery and given the set number 950001.

Bibliography

Bridge, M., *Track Atlas of Mainland Britain*, second edition (Sheffield: Platform 5 Publishing, 2012)

Butcher, A. C., *The Heyday of the DMU* (Shepperton: Ian Allan Publishing, 1994)

Haresnape, B., *British Rail Fleet Survey: 8 Diesel Multiple Units – The First Generation* (Shepperton: Ian Allan Publishing, 1985)

Haresnape, B., *British Rail Fleet Survey: 9 Diesel Multiple Units – The Second Generation and DEMUs* (Shepperton: Ian Allan Publishing, 1986)

Kitchenside, G., *abc British Rail Diesel Multiple Units* (Shepperton: Ian Allan Publishing, 1967)

Pritchard, R., *British Rail Pocket Book No. 3: Diesel Multiple Units 2024* (Sheffield: Platform 5 Publishing, 2023)

Tufnell, R. M., *The British Railcar: AEC to HST* (Newton Abbot: David & Charles, 1984)